Swing
Dance

Swing Dance

Justice O'Connor and the Michigan Muddle

Robert Zelnick

HOOVER INSTITUTION PRESS
Stanford University   Stanford, California

The Hoover Institution on War, Revolution and Peace,
founded at Stanford University in 1919 by Herbert Hoover,
who went on to become the thirty-first president of
the United States, is an interdisciplinary research center
for advanced study on domestic and international affairs.
The views expressed in its publications are entirely those of
the authors and do not necessarily reflect the views of the staff,
officers, or Board of Overseers of the Hoover Institution.

www.hoover.org

Hoover Institution Press Publication No. 528

First printing 2004
10 09 08 07 06 05 04   9 8 7 6 5 4 3 2 1

Manufactured in the United States of America

The paper used in this publication meets the minimum requirements of
the American National Standard for Information Sciences — Permanence
of Paper for Printed Library Materials, ANSI Z39.48-1992. ⊗

Library of Congress Cataloging-in-Publication Data
Zelnick, Robert, 1940–
    Swing dance : Justice O'Connor and the Michigan muddle / by Robert Zelnick.
        p.   cm. — (Hoover Institution Press publication ; no. 528)
    Includes bibliographical references and index.
    ISBN 0-8179-4522-9 (alk. paper)
    1. O'Connor, Sandra Day, 1930–   2. United States. Supreme Court.
3. Universities and colleges — Admission — Law and legislation — Michigan.
4. Discrimination in education — Law and legislation — Michigan.
5. Affirmative action programs — Law and legislation — Michigan.
I. Title.   II. Hoover Institution Press publication ; 528.
KF8742.Z44 2004
344.73'0798 — dc22   2004001433

*Robert Zelnick, an Emmy Award–winning journalist, is a research fellow at the Hoover
Institution and chair of the Department of Journalism at Boston University.*

To Carl Brady,
With Friendship and Gratitude

Contents

Acknowledgments

Once again, my deepest gratitude to John Raisian, director of the Hoover Institution, for his enthusiastic and generous support for this project. Whichever way the cases of *Gratz v. Bollinger* and *Grutter v. Bollinger* came out, John agreed that it would be worthwhile to take a look at the newly redefined status of the law on the subject of race preferences and provide some sense as to which options had been foreclosed and which remained open to the combatants in the arena.

As usual Senior Associate Director Richard Sousa was a big help in getting matters underway. His counsel is uniformly wise; his instincts, sound.

Patricia Baker, executive editor of Hoover Press, took control of the manuscript from the moment of its submission and made certain that it was reviewed in a highly professional manner. I would also like to thank Ann Wood, Senior Editor of the Hoover Institution, and her colleague Tara Joffe for the superb copyediting performed on the original manuscript. The corrections were essential, and the editorial questions and suggestions, quite helpful.

Three researchers were most helpful. Terrence Burlij, at the time an intern with PBS, did a wonderful job pulling together material on the operation of the so-called percentage plans used by California, Texas, and Florida in lieu of race-conscious university admissions procedures, which had been banned by referendum, court decision, or executive order. Zach Altschuler, a law student at Columbia University, provided useful legal research. Katherine McFarland, a law student at Boston University (my own employer), took charge of citations and also suggested several editorial and stylistic changes in the manuscript. In addition, my wife, Pamela, saved me weeks of labor by segregating dozens of pages of quotations from source materials, thus sparing me the burden of reviewing unedited source material from scratch.

My thanks to Carl Cohen, the gifted professor of philosophy at the University of Michigan whose tenacious opposition to race preferences over the course of thirty years has left him with a historical perspective about the issue at Michigan that cannot be matched. The staff at the University of Michigan public affairs office, headed by Deborah Green, was most helpful, as were the good people at the Center for Individual Rights. Both offices, particularly Michigan's, maintain Web sites that provide essential material on the cases. I was prepared to impose on them further, but the more I worked on the project, the more I came to conclude that this is really a story of a legal battle. The more I kept my focus on that battle and the emerging affirmative action law, the more useful my book would be to lawyers, scholars, and interested laypeople alike.

Working on this book, of course, distracted me from some of my duties as chair of the Department of Journalism at Boston University College of Communication. Dean John Schulz and his associate Tobe Berkovitz helped cover my administrative lapses, and the students in my foreign reporting class pretended that nothing whatsoever interfered with my devotion to them.

In the deepest sense, they were right.

Chapter One

The Swing Justice

As the day of reckoning for race-conscious university admissions approached, no one on either side doubted that the issue's fate would rest ultimately with the conscience, the analysis, and the vote of Justice Sandra Day O'Connor. On this issue, as on others such as abortion, states rights, and the *Bush v. Gore* struggle for Florida,[1] O'Connor would find herself neatly positioned between four-justice blocs of liberals and conservatives. This had been substantially true throughout the 1980s, but it was set in concrete in 1991, when the liberal Justice Thurgood Marshall retired and his replacement, the right-wing intellectual Clarence Thomas, was sworn in. During the 1990s, personalities would change as Justices William Brennan and Byron R. White retired, but their liberal replacements, Ruth Bader Ginsburg and Andrew Breyer, preserved the balance. Rarely was Justice O'Connor in the minority on any case. In any given year, scholars could count on the fingers of a single hand the number of times her position in 5-4 splits had failed

---

1. *Bush v. Gore*, 531 U.S. 98 (2000).

to prevail. Now, in anticipating her direction on race-conscious admissions as well as other key issues, commentators would refer to her as the swing vote, the "most powerful woman in America,"[2] or, in the title of a *New York Times Magazine* essay, "A Majority of One."[3]

O'Connor's record on race preference cases produced a good deal of foreboding, even anticipatory anger, among defenders of the approach. "Justice O'Connor is not a swing vote on the Court in matters of racial affirmative action plans as some believe," complained Mercer University law professor Joan Tarpley. "To the contrary, she is the chief architect in dismantling these plans. No less deleterious than Bull Connor's Alabama helmet police and savage dogs were to the 1960s Civil Rights Movement, O'Connor's opinions have dismantled affirmative action programs intended to provide equal economic opportunity to African Americans."[4]

Much of the anger had been initially triggered by O'Connor opinions that had been interpreted at the time as rejecting minority set-asides in government contracting. As early as 1994, Jerome McCristal Culp, Jr., a black law professor at Duke University, complained that by imposing a standard of strict race neutrality on the law, Justice O'Connor was blocking the "Second Reconstruction," just as an earlier brand of reactionary judicial views had blocked the first: "Not only is Justice O'Connor deaf and blind to the concerns of Black Americans—she has, in significant ways, added her

2. Ramesh Ponnuru, *Sandra's Day: Why the Rehnquist Court Has Been the O'Connor Court, and How to Replace Her (Should It Come to That)*, NATIONAL REVIEW, June 30, 2003.

3. Jeffrey Rosen, *A Majority of One*, N.Y. TIMES MAGAZINE, June 2, 2001, §6, at 32.

4. Joan Tarpley, *A Comment on Justice O'Connor's Quest for Power and Its Impact on African American Wealth*, 53 S.C. L. REV. 117, 119 (2001).

voice to form a working majority on the Court in favor of a return to a form of nineteenth-century white supremacy in our judicial discourse on race."[5]

A less angry scholar, Vikram David Amar, of the Hastings College of Law, writing with the benefit of a few years' additional Court pronouncements, saw in O'Connor's work only the command that although, in certain circumstances the government may take race into account, it cannot take *only* race into account. Instead, "Justice O'Connor's basic constitutional admonition is that race ought not to crowd out other aspects of a person's humanity."[6]

Justice Sandra Day O'Connor came to Washington in 1981 as the first Supreme Court justice appointed by Ronald Reagan, who had pledged during his presidential campaign to nominate a woman among his first three Court appointments, and the first woman justice in the history of the Court. She had grown up on her family's Lazy B cattle ranch, a 250-square-mile property on the Arizona–New Mexico border. She graduated from Stanford Law School, where she served as editor of the *Law Review*, dated William Rehnquist, and met her future husband, John O'Connor. Unable because of her sex to land a job with a prestigious law firm, she instead signed on as a county attorney in San Mateo, California, specializing in civil litigation. There followed a period in Germany, where her husband was an Army lawyer, and then private practice in Arizona as well as four years as an assistant attorney general in the state. In 1969, at the age of 39, she was appointed to fill a vacancy in the Arizona senate. She was

5. Jerome McCristal Culp, Jr., *An Open Letter from One Black Scholar to Justice Ruth Bader Ginsburg: Or, How Not to Become Justice Sandra Day O'Connor*, 1 Duke J. Gender L. & Pol'y 21, 22 (1994).

6. Vikram David Amar, *Of Hobgoblins and Justice O'Connor's Jurisprudence of Equality*, 32 McGeorge L. Rev. 823, 826 (2001).

elected on her own in 1970 and was selected Republican majority leader in 1973. Later she served as both a trial and appellate state judge.

At about the time Governor Ronald Reagan was signing a pre–*Roe v. Wade* bill making abortions legal in California, State Senator Sandra Day O'Connor was voting to decriminalize abortions in Arizona. By 1981, both had changed positions, but whereas the right-to-life forces forgave Reagan as the sinner who had seen the light, they didn't trust O'Connor's conversion as real, and many opposed her nomination. Pressed for her views at her confirmation hearings, O'Connor testified, "For myself, abortion is offensive to me, it is repugnant to me, it is something in which I would not engage."[7] In her prepared statement, O'Connor offered only a single matter of substance, telling the committee that her experience as a state legislator "has given me a greater appreciation of the important role the states play in our Federal system, and also a greater appreciation of the separate and distinct roles of the three branches of government at both the state and Federal levels." She also said her experiences "have strengthened my view that the proper role of the judiciary is one of interpreting and applying the law, not making it."[8]

Over her years on the bench, Justice O'Connor would remain far more faithful to the federalism attitude she volunteered than the anti-abortion position articulated in response to committee questions. At the same time, while showing considerable respect for the principle of stare decisis as it pertained to previous Supreme Court decisions, she

7. Eileen McNamara, *Both Sides on Abortion Target O'Connor*, BOSTON GLOBE, June 26, 1989, A1.

8. *Text of Judge O'Connor's Statement to Panel*, N.Y. TIMES, Sept. 10, 1981, at B14.

would become the very antithesis of the judicial self-restraint model her testimony described, tossing out on constitutional grounds acts of Congress, the federal agencies, state and federal courts, and the state legislatures with little apparent hesitation. Legal commentators were slow to discern this propensity in Justice O'Connor's jurisprudence because another of her judicial tendencies was to decide cases on the narrowest of grounds, thereby masking the precedent she was establishing or, more precisely, establishing less precedent than a casual first reading of her opinion might imply. Once the O'Connor pattern became clear, however, critics zeroed in on her "judicial imperiousness." As Jeffrey Rosen complained, "[O'Connor] views the court in general, and herself in particular, as the proper forum to decide every political and constitutional question in the land. And she refuses to defer to competing interpretations by Congress or the state legislatures when they clash with her own."[9]

O'Connor's treatment of the abortion issue would bitterly disappoint those who took seriously her hearing room conversion on the subject. For eight years, she teased them by critiquing both the judicial and medical logic of *Roe* and voting to uphold every state restriction on abortion to come before the bench while postponing an up or down vote on *Roe* and its underlying recognition of unenumerated fundamental rights—in this case, privacy—which the majority had found controlling. She claimed there would be time enough to reconsider *Roe* when the court confronted state laws that were "unduly burdensome" to the exercise of the rights granted in the 1973 decision. When four of her fellow justices thought Missouri had provided the Court with a golden opportunity to reverse *Roe* in the 1989 case of *Webster v.*

9. Rosen, *A Majority of One*, at 32.

Reproductive Health Services,[10] Justice O'Connor, while supporting the Missouri procedures, declined the invitation to take the bigger constitutional step, drawing from Justice Antonin Scalia one of the most wrathful and biting critiques in the recent history of the High Court.[11] Three years later, in *Planned Parenthood of Southeastern Pennsylvania v. Casey*,[12] Justice O'Connor left no doubt that she had crossed the Rubicon on the abortion question, specifically embracing the central holding of *Roe v. Wade*.[13]

It is worth devoting a bit more attention to Justice O'Connor's judicial journey on abortion, because it followed a road very similar to the one she would travel on race preferences. In the 1983 case, *City of Akron v. Akron Center for Reproductive Health*,[14] one of three companion cases dealing with state or local restrictions on abortion, the Court specifically reaffirmed both *Roe* and its trimester approach to abortion regulation. Justice O'Connor dissented in an opinion that urged at least the partial reversal of *Roe*. She termed the trimester system "a completely unworkable method of accommodating the conflicting personal rights and compelling state interests that are involved in the abortion context."[15] Limiting a state's interest to the period when the fetus becomes viable shortchanged the state's interest throughout the pregnancy, because in any stage "there is the potential for human life."[16] Moreover, in terms of science and technol-

---

10. *Webster v. Reproductive Health Services*, 492 U.S. 490 (1989).
11. *Id*. at 532.
12. *Planned Parenthood of Southeastern Pennsylvania v. Casey*, 505 U.S. 833 (1992).
13. *Id*. at 846.
14. *City of Akron v. Akron Center for Reproductive Health*, 462 U.S. 416 (1983).
15. *Id*. at 454.
16. *Id*. at 461.

ogy, *Roe* was on a collision course with itself: "Just as improvements in medical technology inevitably will move *forward* the point at which the State may regulate for reasons of maternal health, different technological improvements will move backward the point of viability at which the State may proscribe abortions except when necessary to preserve the life and health of the mother."[17]

Clearly O'Connor seemed to be positioning herself for the functional, if not total, reversal of *Roe*. State regulations that did not unduly burden a woman's decision to have an abortion would easily pass judicial muster. More severe impediments could be justified by a compelling state need. Because O'Connor seemed to recognize such a need at all stages of the pregnancy, and because the privacy right involved was not absolute, what would be left of *Roe* had her view prevailed on the Court? The moment of truth came in the 1989 *Webster* case, in which a Missouri anti-abortion law came under challenge. The law's preamble stated, "[T]he life of each human being begins at conception," and much of the text of the law was devoted to restrictions against participation in nontherapeutic abortions by public employees and the performance of abortions at public medical facilities or abortions supported by public financing. More important, the legislation also contained a section requiring physicians to test for the viability of a fetus in any pregnancy of twenty weeks or longer and to refrain from performing abortions involving viable fetuses.

A majority of the Supreme Court discarded the preamble challenge as nonsubstantive and the restrictions on public support for abortions as well within the rights of states. How-

17. *Id.* at 456.

ever, a plurality found the viability sections at variance with
Roe's trimester approach. Three justices, led by Chief Justice
Rehnquist, concluded that the *Roe* trimester framework
should be abandoned, a position urged years earlier by Justice
O'Connor. Justice Scalia declared that the time had come to
reverse *Roe*, ending the Court's "self-awarded sovereignty
over a field where it has little proper business since the
answers to most of the cruel questions posed are political and
not juritical—a sovereignty which therefore quite properly,
but to the great damage of the Court, makes it the object of
the sort of organized public pressure that political institutions in a democracy ought to receive."[18]

A number of commentators have suggested that the three
members of the Rehnquist plurality, including Justices White
and Kennedy, were prepared to join Justice Scalia in reversing *Roe*, but they needed a fifth vote, one that Justice
O'Connor refused to provide.[19] Instead, she argued that the
requirement for twenty-week viability determination was not
inconsistent with the trimester approach when the former
was judged a subsidiary matter to be administered only
where not imprudent or careless. "Where there is no need to
decide a constitutional question," she wrote, "it is a venerable principle of this Court's adjudicatory processes not to do
so. . . . Neither will it generally 'formulate a rule of constitutional law that is broader than is required by the precise facts
to which it is to be applied.'"[20]

This sent the former University of Virginia law professor
into judicial orbit. "Justice O'Connor's assertion [citation

---

18. *Webster*, 492 U.S. at 532.

19. *See* Al Kamen & Ruth Marcus, *Two Cases May Clarify O'Connor's Murky Views on Abortion*, Washington Post, Nov. 27, 1989, at A1.

20. *Webster*, 492 U.S. at 490, 525.

omitted] that a 'fundamental rule of judicial restraint' requires us to avoid reconsidering *Roe*, cannot be taken seriously," Scalia huffed.[21] The Missouri case was already being decided on constitutional grounds; the only question was whether, having embarked on the journey, the Court should use *Roe*, its leading case, as a benchmark. According to Scalia, the important principle, then, was not to avoid deciding cases on constitutional grounds; rather, it was to "formulate a rule of constitutional law no broader than is required by the precise facts to which it is applied." And even this "sound general principle" is "often departed from when good reason exists." Indeed, in a recent leading affirmative action opinion written by Justice O'Connor,[22] the Court did not content itself in holding simply that a racially based set-aside was unconstitutional if "unsupported by evidence of identified discrimination"—all that was necessary to decide the case. Instead, "we went on to outline the criteria for properly tailoring race-based remedies in cases where such evidence is present."[23] Justice Scalia then proceeded to cite other examples in which O'Connor opinions reached for constitutional grounds, and having found them, defined them broadly. His tone was one of a superior legal scholar addressing a careless former student whose considerable success cannot be traced to profundity. It caught the attention of a number of commentators and, presumably, did little to endear the Court's first Italian American to its first female. Three years later, in *Planned Parenthood*, Justice O'Connor would join Justices Souter and Kennedy to declare that the principle of stare decisis demanded adherence to the Court's holding in *Roe v. Wade*.

21. *Id.* at 532.
22. *City of Richmond v. J. A. Croson Company*, 488 U.S. 469 (1989).
23. *Webster*, 492 U.S. at 532.

Past reversals by the Court had occurred because of changed facts or appreciation of those facts, they maintained. In Casey, however, where the factual underpinnings of the issue were the same, the Court could not pretend to be reexamining *Roe* with any justification beyond a doctrinal disposition to come out differently from the *Roe* court because that would be an inadequate basis for overruling a prior case.[24]

Justice O'Connor had thus traveled a very long road from the fervent opponent of abortion poised to hold it unconstitutional in the proper case to one who found the right to abortion firmly enough embedded in the law so as not to be overturned without undermining respect for judicial precedent. A scholar examining her opinions would be hard-pressed to see any reversal in terms of specific holding, just a change in tone or emphasis. As would be the case with affirmative action, Justice O'Connor always kept a candle burning in the dark in preparation for the day when she would see the light.

24. *Planned Parenthood*, 505 U.S. at 833, 861.

Chapter Two

Affirmative Action Before O'Connor

Legal challenges to race prefer-
ences can target the actions of private employers (sometimes
prodded by federal agencies), universities and other recipients of government aid, state governments, schools and agencies, or the federal government itself. Where private sector
conduct is involved, the governing law is usually one or more
provisions of the Civil Rights Act of 1964 or less sweeping
later legislation. Alleged government discrimination is most
often challenged under the due process or equal protection
clause of the Fourteenth or Fifth Amendment. Some judges
or justices will provide special deference to acts of Congress
because it is the particular duty of the federal legislature to
implement, by statute, the mandates of the post–Civil War
amendments. By the time Justice Sandra Day O'Connor took
her seat on the nation's highest tribunal to begin her long
march toward primacy in the area of affirmative action jurisprudence, the Court had freshly minted opinions in the three
above areas, which collectively had sanctioned a revolution-
ary lurch in the development of policy from the equal rights,

or "color blind," approach of the 1960s to the subsequent era of race preferences.

The landmark case *California v. Bakke*[1] famously involved the Medical School of the University of California at Davis setting aside 16 places for ethnic minorities from disadvantaged backgrounds in each entering class of 100. Alan Bakke, a practicing engineer whose academic credentials and MCAT performance dwarfed those of the admitted minorities, brought suit challenging the admission practices. The California Supreme Court held in his favor, effectively ordering him admitted and enjoining the school from considering race or ethnicity in its future admissions.[2] The U.S. Supreme Court produced four justices who urged that "benign" acts of race consciousness intended to redress the effects of centuries of past discrimination should be judged leniently,[3] thereby accepting the UC-Davis procedures, and four justices who would have affirmed the state court's decision because, as an institution accepting federal aid, the school was bound by the antidiscrimination provisions of Title VI.[4]

Justice Lewis F. Powell was thus cast in the swing role. Despite the generation of confusion that would grow from his decision, he did accomplish some useful things. First, he disposed of the notion propounded by the four liberal dissenters that a dual standard exists under the Fourteenth Amendment in cases where "benign" discrimination is at issue. "The guarantee of equal protection cannot mean one thing when applied to one individual and something else

---

1. *Regents of the University of California v. Bakke*, 438 U.S. 265 (1978).
2. *Bakke v. Regents of the University of California*, 553 P.2d 1152 (Cal. Sup. Ct. 1976).
3. *Bakke*, 438 U.S. at 272.
4. *Id.* at 409.

when applied to a person of another color," Powell wrote. "If both are not accorded the same protection, then it is not equal." It follows that "[r]acial and ethnic distinctions of any sort are inherently suspect and thus call for the most exacting judicial examination."[5] Under this standard, a person asked by a state to suffer a disadvantage based on race or ethnicity "is entitled to a judgment that the burden he is asked to bear on that basis is precisely tailored to serve a compelling government interest."[6]

Powell also ruled out preferences for minorities that aim to remedy the consequences of historic discrimination or to compensate for the generalized societal discrimination that has not completely been eradicated.[7] He also rejected as unproved the UC-Davis assertion that its quota system was necessary for producing doctors willing to practice in minority neighborhoods.[8] However, he had greater sympathy for the school's claimed need for a diverse student body, saying, "This clearly is a constitutionally permissible goal for an institution of higher education."[9] Indeed, this university's right to build racial, ethnic, or geographic diversity into its program, while not enumerated in the Constitution, was no less precious than other unenumerated First Amendment rights, such as choosing a faculty, developing a curriculum, or determining how its subjects should be taught. "In such an admissions program, race or ethnic background may be deemed a 'plus' in a particular applicant's file, yet it does not insulate the individual from comparison with all other candidates for the available seats," Powell wrote. As a plus factor,

5. *Id.* at 289–290.
6. *Id.* at 299.
7. *Id.* at 310.
8. *Id.* at 307.
9. *Id.* at 312.

it might compare with demonstrated leadership or compassion, a history of overcoming disadvantage, or the ability to communicate with the poor. Indeed, the weight attributed to a particular quality may vary from year to year, depending on the mix of both the student body and the applicants for the incoming class.[10]

Justice Powell gave extraordinary weight to university descriptions of the unquantifiable benefits of their own programs. He cited a report in the *Princeton Alumni Weekly* by President William G. Bowen suggesting that much learning at college occurs informally through interaction among students: "In the nature of things, it is hard to know if this informal 'learning through diversity' actually occurs. It does not occur for everyone. For many, however, the unplanned casual encounters with roommates, fellow sufferers in an organic chemistry class, student workers in the library, teammates on a basketball squad, or other participants in class affairs or student government can be subtle and yet powerful sources of improved understanding and growth."[11]

Powell, a graduate of Harvard Law School, attached as an appendix to his opinion Harvard's description of its own admissions program, which did its best to downplay its reliance on race as simply a little balance-tipper on the scale of rather evenly matched candidates. According to the Harvard document, some candidates are so academically gifted, they demand acceptance, whereas a smaller number are turned away by the Admissions Committee as unqualified: "When the Committee on Admissions reviews the large middle group of applicants who are 'admissible' and deemed capable

---

10. *Id.* at 317.
11. William G. Bowen, *Admissions and the Relevance of Race*, PRINCETON ALUMNI WEEKLY, Sept. 26, 1977, at 7, 9.

of doing good work in their courses, the race of an applicant may tip the balance in his favor just as geographic origin or a life spent on a farm may tip the balance in other candidates' cases. A farm boy from Idaho can bring something to Harvard that a Bostonian cannot offer. Similarly, a black student can usually bring something that a white person cannot offer."[12] Thus was born what might be termed the "Big Lie" about race preferences on campus—the notion that it served mainly as a tiebreaker among applicants of otherwise equal credentials. As statistics, often drawn from downright hostile university administrations would later show, the white-black gaps in terms of SAT and GPA scores were often enormous, particularly at the most selective institutions.

Powell called for the "individualized competitive consideration of race" but gave no reliable guidance as to what specific conduct was ruled in or out. As a result, colleges and universities would deploy a dizzying array of procedures designed to admit large numbers of favored minority candidates, with most such procedures making the mandatory bow to diversity. The University of California at Berkeley, for example, would develop a matrix system that considered GPA and SAT scores along with race, California residence, and other social and academic factors, which together magically produced a nearly identical percentage of blacks and Hispanics in class after class. The University of Texas Law School maintained separate color-coded files for white and minority candidates, along with separate "presumptively admit" and "presumptively reject" scores that favored minority applicants. The University of Georgia, later joined by the University of Michigan, added twenty points to a candidate's application score based solely on race or ethnicity. Michi-

---

12. *Bakke*, 438 U.S. at 316.

gan's law school, after years of mandated preferences, adopted a so-called critical mass objective, which—through unabashed preferences—produced classes with 10 to 17 percent preferred minority enrollment year in and year out.[13]

The glowing accounts of admissions practices by Harvard and Princeton proved to have little basis in fact, at least with respect to most admissions programs. Rather than a tiebreaker between two otherwise evenly matched candidates from the "large middle group of applicants," race instead became a decisive attribute, vaulting blacks and Hispanics with marginal academic credentials over whites and Asian Americans with far more impressive records. Under UC-Davis's challenged quotas, Bakke had scores of 96, 94, 97, and 72 on the verbal, quantitative, science, and general information sections of his MCAT exams, while the comparable scores of the "special admitees" were 34, 30, 37, and 18, respectively.[14] Under systems purporting to follow Justice Powell's command, the results were little different. Year in and year out, for example, the average MCAT scores of admitted African American and Hispanic candidates were lower than the average scores of rejected whites and Asian Americans. In the more selective schools, the average SAT difference between whites and blacks approached or exceeded 200 points. High school GPA gaps were similarly wide. Predictably, those minorities admitted on "diversity" grounds did rather poorly in class. Their dropout rates were far higher than regularly admitted students, and they tended to congregate toward the bottom of their college classes.[15]

13. Report and Recommendations of the Admissions Committee, University of Michigan Law School (April 24, 1992).

14. *Bakke*, 438 U.S. at 277.

15. Thomas E. Wood & Malcolm J. Sherman, *Race and Higher Education* (National Association of Scholars, May 2001); Robert Lerner & Althea K. Nagai, *A*

Race-conscious admission practices in the service of "diversity" also raise some troubling issues in the context of affirmative action law. Paramount among these issues is that the practice pretends to be a device for providing better, more complete education for all students. Rather it is much more a device for compensating minorities for historic and societal discrimination. Universities have long practiced diversity admissions, but no one ever pretended that one needed 10 or 15 percent Idaho farmers or oboe players to tap adequately into the contribution they make. Nor has anyone ever pretended that any of these farmers or musicians would be at the elite school in question with SAT scores 200 points below the median. At no elite campus is there a strata of farmers, flutists, or even legatees readily identifiable, self-segregated, shunning most of the more challenging career paths, and still on the academic floor of the institution. In addition, as has become more and more clear, the program of race-conscious admissions knows no boundaries of time. Because the purported need is based on educational values rather than justice and, as mentioned, benefits students of all races, the only occurrence that would terminate the practice would be the sudden appearance of a field of minorities as qualified as the white or Asian American student populations. Just as a black child born in 1978, the year of *Bakke*, has made little progress in closing the academic gap favoring whites, so too will the minority child born today almost certainly be in a similar predicament vis-à-vis whites a generation hence.

At the time *Bakke* was decided, the lyrical tributes offered regarding the pedagogical benefits of diversity were largely

---

Critique of the Expert Report of Patricia Gurin in Gratz v. Bollinger (available at www.ceousa.org).

theoretical, perhaps even theological. Instead of "informal learning through diversity," what many schools actually experienced was the division of students along racial lines segregated by housing, culture, even academic pursuit; the stigmatizing effects of their marginal academic performance on the beneficiaries of affirmative action; a developing practice of grade inflation designed in part to conceal the showing of these preferred minorities; and the evolution of a campus environment shrouded in myth and disinformation and regulated by speech code. What would happen if it were shown that the admissions procedures licensed by *Bakke* didn't work, that they disserved academic values and produced less desirable educational outcomes? Would the colleges and universities alter their course? Would they implement reverse affirmative action programs designed to reduce the number of minorities on campus? Would they at least revert to merit-based systems, which would limit admissions to those whose presence could be justified solely on academic grounds? Or would they simply switch their propaganda machines into overdrive, churning out volumes of new academic fluff designed to obscure, rather than illuminate, the truth?

In the quarter century after the *Bakke* decision, the Court decided nearly a dozen affirmative action cases, many of considerable importance. Until it revisited the *Bakke* question, however, its treatment of the issue seemed incomplete.

The Supreme Court Sanctions Preferences

During the era of official racial segregation in the South and widespread employment discrimination elsewhere, craft unions frequently excluded black workers from membership, thereby restricting access to higher-paying skilled factory jobs and limiting them mainly to unskilled production line positions. At the Kaiser Aluminum & Chemical Corp. plant in Gramercy, Louisiana, for example, 39 percent of the workforce was black, but only 5 out of 273 craft positions—1.83 percent—were held by blacks.[16] Following creation of the Equal Employment Opportunities Commission by the Civil Rights Act of 1964, the agency began zeroing in on the Gramercy plant, demanding that Kaiser take steps to redress the gross racial imbalance. In response to this pressure, Kaiser reached accord with the United Steelworkers of America (USWA) whereby the company would cease hiring outsiders for craftsman vacancies and would instead train workers inside the plant. Blacks would participate in the program at a rate of 50 percent until the percentage of skilled black workers mirrored their percentage in the local labor force. Blacks selected for the program often had less seniority than rejected whites. Weber, one of the whites left out of the program, challenged the deal as a violation of the Civil Rights Act of 1964, which forbids job discrimination by large employers on the basis of race.

Weber's point was "not without force," conceded Justice William J. Brennan, writing for the majority. "But it overlooks the significance of the fact that the Kaiser-USWA plan is an affirmative action plan voluntarily adopted by private parties to eliminate traditional patterns of racial segregation."[17] Moreover, to resolve questions regarding the specific language of the bill, the Court must examine the overall intent of Congress, which was to improve the economic plight of black Americans. As Senator Hubert H. Humphrey offered

16. *United Steelworkers v. Weber*, 443 U.S. 193, 198 (1979).
17. *Id.* at 201.

during the debate, "What good does it do a Negro to be able to eat in a fine restaurant if he cannot afford to pay the bill?"[18]

To reach the Court's decision approving Kaiser's deal with the steelworkers union, Justice Brennan had to deal with the mildly inconvenient language of Section 703(j) of Title VII, which said that nothing contained in the title "shall be interpreted to require any employer . . . to grant preferential treatment to any group because of the race . . . of such group . . . on account of a de facto imbalance in the employer's work force." Justice Brennan concluded, however, that this section, which was added to win or maintain support from legislators in both houses of Congress "who traditionally resisted federal regulation of private business," could not be interpreted as banning voluntary private accords, even those made under federal pressure.[19]

However, the majority ignored a far more explicit provision of Title VII, Section 703(d), which provides that "[i]t shall be an unlawful employment practice for any employer, labor organization, or joint labor-management committee controlling apprenticeship or other training or retraining, including on-the-job training programs, to discriminate against any individual because of his race, color, religion, sex, or national origin in admission to or employment in any program established to provide apprenticeship or other training."[20] A second section, 703(a)(2), contained similar language with respect to employer practices.

In a brutal, comprehensive dissent in which he exhaustively reviewed the legislative history of Title VII, Justice Rehnquist, joined by Chief Justice Warren E. Burger, accused

18. *Id.* at 203.
19. *Id.* at 206.
20. *Id.*

the majority of an Orwellian propensity for twisting the plain meaning of the act's provisions and the interpretations of those provisions offered during the many weeks of floor debate in both houses.[21] Rehnquist was questioning neither redress to black workers for a century of acknowledged discrimination nor what Congress should have included in the bill. Rather he questioned what Congress specifically enacted and how those authoring the legislation explained its provisions. Clearly compromises had to be made to secure passage. However, one of the compromises explicitly written into the legislation prevented compensatory relief for black victims of employment discrimination before such discrimination had been outlawed by passage of the act. Justice Rehnquist cited the words of Representative Emanuel Cellar, chair of the House Judiciary Committee and principal author of Title VII: "Even [a] court could not order that any preference be given to any particular race, religion or other group, but would be limited to ordering an end of discrimination."[22]

On the Senate side, Senator Hubert Humphrey confirmed that "nothing in the bill would permit any official or court to require any employer or labor union to give preferential treatment to any minority group."[23] There were dozens of similar statements, many by the bill's principal sponsors. Senators Joseph Clark and Clifford Casse, for example, were the two "floor captains" for the legislation. In a memorandum for the record, they offered the following: "Title VII would have no effect on established seniority rights. Its effect is prospective and not retrospective. Thus, for example, if a business has been discriminating in the past and as a result has an all-

---

21. *Id.* at 221.
22. *Id.* at 233.
23. *Id.* at 237.

white work force, when the title comes into effect the employer's obligation would be simply to fill future vacancies on a nondiscriminatory basis. He would not be obliged—or indeed permitted—to fire whites in order to hire Negroes, or, once Negroes are hired, to give them special seniority rights at the expense of white workers hired earlier."[24]

In fact, until it was embraced by the Supreme Court, no contrary interpretation was offered by any legislator. Southerners and other conservative opponents worried about federal regulators and the courts, but not about voluntary actions by employers and unions. In Justice Rehnquist's words, "Not once during the 83 days of debate in the Senate did a speaker, proponent or opponent, suggest that the bill would allow employers voluntarily to prefer racial minorities over white persons."[25]

Again, the majority decision in *Weber* was more an affront to principles involving the separation of powers than those involving racial justice. Surely employment discrimination against blacks had been egregious and had produced a national calamity of unemployment, underemployment, poverty, hopelessness, and despair. What better way to bring large numbers of minorities into the economic mainstream than to accelerate their acquisition of skills through on-the-job training and apprenticeship programs. However, by twisting the meaning of the bill's clear language and by distorting the legislative history to reach the result favored by a majority of the Court, the justices contributed to the notion—already evident in *Bakke* and college admissions—that those on the side of compensatory justice for blacks were engaged in a noble, deeply moral, almost holy battle that created, and had

24. *Id.* at 240.
25. *Id.* at 244.

to be judged by, its own standards. This cause took its legitimacy not from traditional notions of truth, nor academic integrity, nor intellectual consistency, but rather from the ugliness of the original sin and its lingering effects upon the national soul. Thus, a form of super morality came into play, one that continues to invest the cause of racial justice, or perhaps to infect it.

Government Set-asides

Fullilove v. Klutznick[26] was the last of the pre-O'Connor affirmative action cases and the first to deal with the question of government set-asides. The law that would trigger decades of debate began almost by stealth, as Representative Clarence Mitchell in the House and Senator Edward Brooke in the Senate successfully introduced floor amendments into the Public Works Employment Act of 1977.[27] The amendments required the Department of Commerce to ensure that at least 10 percent of federal funds allocated for local public works projects went to companies owned and controlled by minorities, in this case blacks, Hispanics, Asians, and Native American Indians, Eskimos, and Aleuts. White contractors challenged the minority business enterprise (MBE) provision for violating the due process clause of the Fifth Amendment and Title VI of the Civil Rights Act of 1964.

Just as his judicial philosophy of self-restraint had compelled his dissent from the massive legislative rewrite job undertaken by the Court in *Weber*, so too did it dictate Chief Justice Burger's acquiescence to the legislation under challenge in *Fullilove*. Congress, he wrote, had special responsi-

---

26. *Fullilove v. Klutznick*, 448 U.S. 448 (1980).
27. *Public Works Employment Act*, Pub. L. 95-28, 91 *Stat.* 116 (1977).

bility for implementing the post–Civil War constitutional amendments. There was ample evidence that minorities were suffering from the present effects of past discrimination. The minorities in question accounted for 16 percent of the nation's population but only owned 3 percent of its businesses. In 1976, less than 1 percent of state and federal contracting was performed with MBEs.[28] "The presumption must be made that past discriminatory systems have resulted in present economic inequities,"[29] Justice Burger wrote. Just as race-conscious steps had been needed to redress the effects of a century of school segregation, according to Burger, "[W]e reject the contention that in the remedial context the Congress must act in a wholly 'color-blind' fashion."[30]

Justice Burger's decision was flabby and vague. His avuncular judicial personality beamed unwarranted benevolence toward an action of facially questionable legality, particularly as it had sprung full grown from two floor amendments. What was the evidence of discrimination? Did the law really apply to groups like Aleuts, a community of hunters and fishers whose affinity for the construction business had been historically well concealed? Did Asians, with their high rates of business formation and documented zest for education and self-improvement, truly fit with the others? What about exploring race-neutral measures—mentoring programs, joint venture projects with more established firms, the waiver of default bonding requirements to mention just three—which could be of lasting benefit to minority contractors?

Justice Powell's concurring opinion, concluding "that the Enforcement Clauses of the Thirteenth and Fourteenth

---

28. *Fullilove*, 448 U.S. at 465.
29. *Id.*
30. *Id.* at 482.

Amendments confer upon Congress the authority to select reasonable remedies to advance the compelling state interest in repairing the effects of past discrimination,"[31] provided an additional voice to Burger's but not the missing steel.

In his dissent, Justice Potter Stewart invoked the words of Justice John Harlan in his historic *Plessy v. Ferguson* dissent: "Our Constitution is color-blind, and neither knows nor tolerates classes among citizens."[32] The country's tortured racial history contains a single paramount lesson: "The color of a person's skin and the country of his origin bear no relation to ability, disadvantage, moral culpability, or any other characteristics of constitutionally permissible interest to government."[33] Justice Stewart, a respected and independent voice, soon died of cancer. His fellow dissenter in *Fullilove*, Justice Rehnquist, would a bit later be elevated to Chief Justice, where he would attempt to cobble together new majorities for his views on a variety of issues, including affirmative action.

It could well have been argued at the time Justice O'Connor succeeded to the Court that the affirmative action issue was moot. *Bakke* had offered colleges and universities a safe harbor for race-conscious admissions programs so long as they were carefully developed. *Weber* had opened the door to voluntary "diversity" programs in business and industry despite the rich legislative history rejecting all forms of race or ethnic preferences. Finally, government set-asides had become the law of the land. For Sandra Day O'Connor to make her mark as a jurist, surely it would be in some other area of the law.

31. *Id.* at 510.
32. *Id.* at 522.
33. *Id.*

Chapter Three

O'Connor and the Employment Cases

Justice O'Connor's debut in the affirmative action field was modest. In the 1984 case of *Firefighters Local Union No. 1784 v. Stotts*,[1] the Court reversed a district court order invalidating the operation of a seniority system, negotiated between the firefighters union and the city of Memphis, that would have protected many white veteran firefighters against more recently hired blacks during a period of budget-induced layoffs. In an earlier consent decree reached with blacks claiming discrimination in hiring and promotion, the fire department, though not conceding discrimination, had committed itself to nondiscriminatory future practices. Firefighters Local No. 1784 had not been privy to those negotiations, and the agreement itself had made no specific mention of the seniority system or any other action that would have been injurious to existing employees. Thus, the district court's modification of the consent decree was supported neither by a robust record of discrimination

---

1. *Firefighters Local Union No. 1784 v. Stotts*, 467 U.S. 561 (1984).

nor by inclusion of the organization representing parties likely to be injured by the decree.

The Court held that Section 703(h) of Title VII of the Civil Rights Act insulates bona fide seniority systems save for the actual victims of past discrimination. Writing for the majority, Justice White suggested, "If individual members of a plaintiff class demonstrate that they have been actual victims of the discriminatory practice, they may be awarded competitive seniority and given their rightful place on the seniority roster."[2] The remaining members of the plaintiff class were entitled to no special protection. The Court recalled Senator Humphrey's words during floor debate on the legislation: "No court order can require hiring, reinstatement, admission to membership, or payment of back pay for anyone who was not fired, refused employment or advancement or admission to a union by an act of discrimination forbidden by this title."[3]

Justice O'Connor wrote a short gratuitous concurrence, like a recruit already part of the formation announcing her presence after the roll has been called. However, in 1986, *Wygant v. Jackson*[4] provided the Court and Justice O'Connor with the opportunity to define their respective approaches toward affirmative action in ways that would be reflected in many later decisions.

Just as tough cases are said to make bad law, *Stotts* showed that easy cases may sometimes make incomplete law. The glaring question left unanswered by *Stotts* was whether, given a pervasive or egregious pattern of documented discrimination by a union or an employer, the courts could order

---

2. *Id.* at 578–579.
3. *Id.* at 580.
4. *Wygant v. Jackson Board of Education*, 476 U.S. 267 (1986).

forms of relief unavailable to redress innocent racial or ethnic imbalances. Such relief could extend preferential treatment to minority group members who had not themselves suffered discrimination, or it could involve hiring quotas. The Court would begin to put some meat on the skeletal *Stotts* case two years later in the important *Wygant* case.

During a period of racial tensions in the early 1970s, the Jackson, Michigan, Board of Education reached agreement with the local teachers union that, should it become necessary to lay off teachers, seniority rights would be observed except that at no time would there be a greater percentage of minority teachers laid off than the percentage of minority teachers employed at the time of the layoffs. When layoffs did occur, the board implemented the accord, laying off several nonminority teachers while retaining minority teachers with less seniority. Laid-off white teachers then filed suit, claiming the action of the board violated the equal protection clause of the Fourteenth Amendment as well as Title VII of the Civil Rights Act. In the lower federal courts, the board said the purpose of the agreement was to keep the percentage of minority teachers about the same as minority students to provide role models for the latter, an action made necessary by the long history of societal discrimination against black people. Although no history of racial discrimination was ever found on the part of the Jackson school system, both lower courts held the policy of redressing societal discrimination through the provision of role models permissible, and the means employed, reasonable.[5] The Supreme Court reversed the decision.[6]

Although he could not succeed in attracting five justices

5. 546 F. Supp. 1195 (E.D. Mich. 1982); 746 F.2d 1152 (6th Cir. 1984).
6. *Wygant*, 476 U.S. at 273.

to his plurality decision, Justice Powell authored an opinion rich in axioms that would become the lore of the land in affirmative action jurisprudence. Justice O'Connor, in her concurrence, provided a good look at her early approach to the issue plus what seems, in retrospect, a rather optimistic belief that consensus on the Court could be found on this divisive national question.

Justice Powell declared that race-conscious policies must be invoked only to redress specific past discrimination: "Societal discrimination, without more, is too amorphous a basis for imposing a racially classified remedy."[7] The effort to find role models cannot be used to support discriminatory layoffs because it bears no necessary relationship to past hiring practices. In fact, were there only a small number of minority children in the schools but a high percentage of black teachers in the labor pool, pegging the number of black teachers to the percentage of minority students could actually create discrimination in hiring. Further, a finding of past discrimination would provide an anchor for what otherwise might be wildly adrift remedies: "In the absence of particularized findings, a court could uphold remedies that are ageless in the reach into the past, and timeless in their ability to affect the future."[8]

Justice Powell did not find the remedy narrowly tailored, even had the policy objective been lawful.[9] In addition, while the Court looks closely at all race-conscious actions, it casts an especially skeptical eye on those that rely upon dismissals or abrogated seniority arrangements to achieve their ends. A worker applying for a job (or a student applying for college)

---

7. *Id.* at 276.
8. *Id.*
9. *Id.* at 283.

may have a hope but no reasonable expectation of acceptance, but a worker with accumulated seniority owns something of value potentially more precious than the title to a
home. "While hiring goals impose a diffuse burden, often
foreclosing only one of several opportunities, layoffs impose
the entire burden of achieving racial equality on particular
individuals, often resulting in serious disruption of their
lives."[10]

In her concurrence, Justice O'Connor first searched for
common ground regarding the test to which racial classifications are subjected. The standard is "strict scrutiny"—not
"strict in theory and fatal in fact," but "strict and searching."[11]
She saw Justice Powell translating this into requirements that
"(1) the racial classification be justified by a 'compelling governmental interest,' and (2) the means chosen by the state to
effectuate its purpose be 'narrowly tailored.'"[12] She found
transient comments from the pro-affirmative action justices
suggesting that they too favored strict scrutiny; but then she
recalled their argument in *Bakke* that "remedial use of race
is permissible if it serves 'important governmental objectives'
and is 'substantially related to achievement of those objectives.'"[13] This was a far more tolerant standard, but one that
had already set one Court faction apart from the other and
would do so for years to come. However, O'Connor suggested
than in many situations the difference in framing the issue
"may be a negligible one."[14] Having blithely sought unity
where disunity reigned, Justice O'Connor announced her
own position: "I subscribe to Justice Powell's formulation

10. *Id.* at 283.
11. *Id.* at 285.
12. *Id.* at 287.
13. *Id.*
14. *Id.*

because it mirrors the standard we have consistently applied in examining racial classifications in other contexts."[15]

Still, she invited conciliation. Redressing specific past discrimination is one path toward race-conscious solutions, but there are others as well: "[A]lthough its precise contours are uncertain, a state interest in the promotion of racial diversity has been found sufficiently 'compelling,' at least in the context of higher education, to support the use of racial classifications in furthering that interest. And nothing the Court has said today necessarily forecloses the possibility that the Court will find other governmental interests which have been relied upon in the lower courts but which have not been passed on here to be sufficiently 'important' or 'compelling' to sustain the use of affirmative action policies."[16]

So we see here what appears to be at least a passive endorsement of *Bakke*, a position Justice O'Connor would never expressly disavow, though her opinions in other cases would lead opponents of race preferences to conclude she had cast aside the rationale for Justice Powell's opinion. At the time of *Wygant*, however, Justice O'Connor was still trying to find common ground with Justices Marshall, Brennan, and Blackmun. Although a state cannot get into the business of race consciousness without the trigger of its own past discrimination, "it is agreed that a plan need not be limited to the remedying of specific instances of identified discrimination for it to be deemed sufficiently 'narrowly tailored' or 'substantially related' to the correction of prior discrimination by the state actor."[17] This is not something Powell dealt with in his opinion, and it reflects a recurrent tendency in

15. *Id*. at 285.
16. *Id*.
17. *Id*. at 287.

Justice O'Connor's work of limiting and narrowing a Court decision even while purporting to concur with it.

Justice O'Connor next embraced Powell's conclusion that societal discrimination "cannot be deemed sufficiently compelling to pass constitutional muster under strict scrutiny" and that the "role model" rationale must fail.[18] In an important qualification, however, barely noticed at the time, she volunteered the sort of evidence that state defenders of race-conscious programs might offer to justify their remedy: "[D]emonstrable evidence of a disparity between the percentage of qualified blacks on a school's teaching staff and the percentage of qualified minorities in the relevant labor pool sufficient to support a prima facie Title VII pattern or practice claim by minority teachers would lend a compelling basis for a competent authority such as the School Board to conclude that implementation of a voluntary affirmative action plan is appropriate to remedy apparent employment discrimination."[19]

The notion of disparity studies to document discrimination was borrowed from the controversial world of the Equal Employment Opportunity Commission (EEOC) and related agencies investigating companies' compliance with federal nondiscrimination law. Often, in the absence of documented discriminatory practices, testing, or other requirements having a "disparate impact" on minorities, the regulators would fall back on statistics showing a disparity between the percentage of minority workers at a given establishment versus the percentage of minority members of the relevant labor force. Should it appear that minorities were "underrepresented" at the establishment in question, the

18. *Id.* at 288.
19. *Id.* at 291.

agency would put its enforcement mechanisms into play, ranging from simple findings of noncompliance to suspension of government contractors to the requirement that the employer promptly devise and implement an affirmative action plan. In *Wygant*, Justice O'Connor suggested applying this doctrine to potential race-conscious programs by the state. She raised the issue again when she wrote the opinion of the Court in the *Croson* case, which at first reading seemed to ban race set-asides in state contracts but which led to the introduction of hundreds of state "disparity studies" justifying continued set-asides. When it came to escaping from the central thrust of her own decrees, Justice O'Connor had few peers on her bench, or on any other.

Stretching the Civil Rights Act

On July 2, 1986, the Court decided two cases that pushed affirmative action in employment well into the gray areas of the Civil Rights Act of 1964, if not beyond. As was by then her custom, Justice O'Connor placed her individual views into the record in each case, concurring in one, dissenting in substantial part in the other.

Firefighters Local 93 v. Cleveland[20] began as a lawsuit by Vanguard—an association of black and Hispanic Cleveland firefighters claiming discrimination in hiring, assigning, and promoting minorities, including the use of culturally biased standardized tests. The city, which had resisted and lost two recent discrimination suits involving both the police and fire departments, was in no mood to again be adjudged harshly. Therefore, it negotiated with Vanguard a consent decree call-

20. *International Association of Firefighters v. City of Cleveland*, 478 U.S. 501 (1986).

ing for specific numbers of minority candidates to be lieuten-
ant, captain, battalion chief, and assistant chief. Under the
agreement, "appropriate minority hiring goals" were to be
established for future promotions, with the city refraining
from using seniority points in promotions. The plan, which
was to remain in effect for nine years, could be extended for
an additional six years by agreement. Firefighters Local 93
had been excluded from the talks, and when it objected to
the deal, the district court judge proposed boosting the number of planned promotions so that whites would actually
wind up with more promotions than without affirmative
action. Still the union membership voted overwhelmingly
against the plan. A revised consent decree, not too dissimilar
to the one rejected by Local 93, was eventually approved by
the district court, which found from earlier municipal hearing records abundant evidence of past discrimination—much
of it admitted by the department—and affirmed on appeal.[21]

The issue before the Court was whether the lower court
could enter a consent decree that provided remedies beyond
ones the court could have ordered under the Civil Rights Act
following an adversary proceeding. Without question, Section 706(g) of the act prohibited courts from ordering reinstatement of a union member or the "hiring, reinstatement or
promotion of an individual as an employee, or the payment
to him of any back pay" if that person had been "refused
employment or advancement or was suspended or dis-
charged for any reason other than discrimination on account
of race, color, religion, sex, or national origin."[22] In other
words, unless one had been the victim of direct racial, ethnic,

21. *Id.* at 501–511.
22. 42 U.S.C. 2000d et seq. (1964) (amended by Civil Rights Act of 1991, 42
U.S.C. 2000e et seq. (1991)).

nationality, or gender discrimination, he or she could not benefit from mere membership in a group that had suffered discrimination.

In this case, the Court majority stretched a bit. Recalling the "voluntary" contract—albeit under EEOC pressure—that Kaiser had reached with the Steelworkers Union in the *Weber* case, the Court concluded that consent decrees were, for purposes of affirmative action, more like the contract in *Weber* than the traditional judicial order subject to Civil Rights Act limitation. After all, Congress preferred voluntary rather than coerced employer action. Thus, wrote Justice Brennan for a six-justice majority, the act "does not restrict the ability of employers or unions to enter into voluntary agreements providing for race-conscious remedial action."[23]

In her concurring opinion, Justice O'Connor sought to narrow the holding's applicability—a familiar propensity. Yes, the parties can negotiate a consent decree beyond what a court could impose after a contested case. However, injured nonparties could still challenge the accord under other sections of the act or even under the Fourteenth Amendment.[24] Moreover, if previous holdings suggest that an employer's prior discriminatory conduct "is the necessary predicate for a 'temporary remedy favoring black employees,'" the Court's opinion would leave that requirement "wholly undisturbed."[25]

The combination of *Weber* and *Firefighters* pushed the possibilities of affirmative action in a direction sponsors of the act had assured colleagues it would not go—toward an employer's "voluntary" agreement to implement hiring or

23. *Firefighters*, 478 U.S. at 511.
24. *Id.* at 530.
25. *Id.* at 531.

promotional "goals" to benefit blacks or Hispanics who had not themselves been victims of discrimination by the employer in question, even though that employer may have been utterly racist in its hiring or promotional practices. Of course, the employer's conduct may have been considerably more benign and the consent decree simply a practical way to avoid years of costly and damaging litigation.

Local 28 of the Sheet Metal Workers International Association v. Equal Employment Opportunity Commission,[26] decided the same day as *Firefighters v. Cleveland*, took another giant step in the direction of a body of substantive discrimination law developed by judicial decision rather than by legislative process. The case began with a suit by the U.S. Department of Justice, succeeded by the EEOC, to enjoin the New York–based craft union and its apprenticeship program from engaging in a pattern and practice of discrimination against nonwhites. The district court found pervasive violations of the Civil Rights Act in the recruitment, selection, training, and admission to the union and, following continued union resistance to change its ways, established a 29 percent "goal" for nonwhite union membership. This figure was a reflection of the percentage of blacks in the relevant labor pool. The district court also ordered a union affirmative action program recommended by a court-appointed administrator. Following an appeal, lost by the union, the district court twice held the union in contempt for deliberately failing to implement the required changes, slightly increasing the target percentage for nonwhite workers and directing that fines for contempt levied against the union be placed in a

---

26. *Local 28 of the Sheet Metal Workers International Association v. Equal Employment Opportunity Commission*, 478 U.S. 421 (1986).

fund devoted to increasing nonwhite union membership.[27] The court further relaxed the initial timetable in response to union complaints that it was the sluggish economy of the early 1980s, rather than its own malevolence, keeping minority numbers low. Affirmed on appeal, the case came to the Supreme Court and raised the question of whether, even in response to egregious discrimination, the wording and history of the Civil Rights Act permitted a court to order a functional quota as a vehicle for relief and whether a court could implement a race-conscious plan of direct benefit to many who had not been victims of discrimination.

Writing for the majority, Justice Brennan first held that the Civil Rights Act "does not prevent a court from ordering, in appropriate circumstances, affirmative race-conscious relief as a remedy for past discrimination . . . where an employer or a labor union has engaged in persistent or egregious discrimination, or where necessary to dissipate the lingering effects of pervasive discrimination."[28] In addition, Section 706(g)—which denies compensatory relief to individuals not subject to racial or ethnic discrimination—does not stop a court "from ordering affirmative race-conscious relief which might incidentally benefit individuals who were not the actual victims of discrimination."[29] Rather the intent of the section, according to Brennan, was to deny relief to someone a union could prove would not have gotten the job anyway, even with no discrimination. In cases of long-standing or egregious discrimination, however, Brennan averred it may be that only a firm goal that requires the hiring of minorities in rough proportion to their place in the relevant

27. *Id.* at 430–436.
28. *Id.* at 445.
29. *Id.*

work force would break the pattern of endless evasion and litigation. Such an order would reinforce the principal congressional objective—"to open employment opportunities to Negroes in occupations which have been traditionally closed to them."[30] Simply stopping discrimination may not be enough to attract minority job applicants when the employer's long-standing reputation is of one with doors closed to minorities. Affirmative action erases the "outward and visible signs of yesterday's racial distinctions" in a way necessary to attract potential black employees.[31] Numerical goals may also be an important judicial tool for reducing the effects of past discrimination. In short, as the lower federal courts had unanimously held, "[R]acial preferences may be used, in appropriate cases, to remedy past discrimination under Title VII."[32] The union and the EEOC (during the Reagan years, the EEOC took some conservative positions before the Supreme Court) were wrong to conclude that the act prevented nonvictims from participating in the mediation of past discrimination. Congress only sought to demand that "an employer would not violate the statute merely by having a racially imbalanced work force, and consequently, that a court could not order an employer to adopt racial preferences merely to correct such an imbalance."[33]

The Court noted the refusal of Congress, when considering the Equal Employment Opportunity Act of 1972, to pass two amendments that would have explicitly limited relief to proven victims of discrimination. The Court also expressed confidence that the 29 percent goal established by the lower

30. *Id.* at 448.
31. *Id.* at 450.
32. *Id.* at 451.
33. *Id.* at 453.

court would prove flexible in practice and that both it and the fund established with contempt fines would dissolve once the system had been purged of past discrimination.[34]

Justice O'Connor dissented sharply from the acceptance by the majority of the combination 29 percent goal and fund order, claiming that the goal thereby becomes "a rigid racial quota" barred by the 1964 act.[35] Congress sought to preclude quotas because of the harm they would impose on innocent nonminority workers and "the restriction on employer freedom that would follow from an across-the-board requirement of racial balance in every workplace."[36] She was not shutting the door on "racial preferences short of quotas," but even these preferences should be used when clearly necessary only if they would benefit nonvictims at the expense of victims.

Justice O'Connor was by that time—not uncharacteristically—walking an extremely fine line. References to the percentages of minority workers in a given labor pool were useful, but only as benchmarks "to estimate how an employer's work force would be composed absent past discrimination."[37] One cannot assume, however, that people of the various races "will gravitate with mathematical exactitude to each employer or union absent unlawful discrimination." Therefore, there must be "a substantial statistical disparity between the composition of an employer's work force and the relevant labor pool, or the general population, before an intent to discriminate may be inferred from such a disparity."[38]

34. *Id.* at 482.
35. *Id.* at 489.
36. *Id.* at 493.
37. *Id.* at 494.
38. *Id.*

To be consistent with the act, a racial hiring or membership goal "must be intended to serve merely as a benchmark for measuring compliance with Title VII and eliminating the lingering effects of past discrimination, rather than as a rigid numerical requirement that must unconditionally be met on pain of sanctions," according to Justice O'Connor. A permissible goal "should require only a good-faith effort on the employer's or union's part to come within a range demarcated by the goal itself."[39]

This was all well and good in the abstract, but the Court was dealing with a union with a history of racial exclusion that violated New York state law even before passage of the Civil Rights Act of 1964, a union that showed a pervasive, persistent, and egregious refusal to comply with the law. No labor force benchmarks were needed in this instance because the number of black craftsmen taken into the union was close to zero. When confronted with judicial orders to end such practices, the union's lack of good faith was such that it was twice held in civil contempt. So, for all its insistent language, the O'Connor dissent never grappled with the question of what to do with a union or employer that acts in bad faith, contrary to law and court order, and that does so repeatedly. Is this actor to be treated with soft "goals" and benchmarks to measure its "good faith," or does it need a hard standard, subject to judicial amelioration, should circumstances change—as happened when the economy went south in the early 1980s and the federal district court extended the compliance deadline? Justice O'Connor was still finding her own way on affirmative action cases, still grasping for a rule of reason as crisp and logical as Justice Powell's notion of com-

39. *Id.* at 495.

pelling interest and narrow tailoring. In the *Sheet Metal Workers* case, she had still not found it.

United States v. Paradise,[40] decided in February 1987, also involved a court-ordered remedy for wanton racial discrimination, this time practiced by an agency of the state, and another dissent by Justice O'Connor that, like the *Sheet Metal Workers* case, seemed to be applying the right standard to the wrong set of facts.

The case grew out of a lawsuit originally filed in 1972 in which the NAACP charged the Alabama Department of Public Safety with illegally refusing to hire blacks. The case, tried before legendary District Court Judge Frank M. Johnson, was open and shut; in the 37-year history of the department, not a single black had ever been hired as a state trooper or for any but the most menial of jobs. Endeavoring to end not only the discrimination itself but also its present effects, Judge Johnson ordered the department to hire one black trooper for each white until 25 percent of the force—roughly equivalent to the percentage of blacks in the relevant labor force—was black and to develop recruitment, examination, training, promotion, and other personnel policies that neither in purpose nor effect discriminated against blacks.[41]

Evidence that developed during the litigation proved that, at least in the early years, the department sought to evade its responsibility. At first, the department perceived a vastly scaled-back need for new troopers, thus minimizing the number of blacks brought onto the force. Some blacks were eventually hired, but personnel policies were administered unevenly and little effort was made to develop fair promotion

40. *United States v. Paradise*, 480 U.S. 149 (1987).
41. 317 F. Supp. 1079 (M.D. Ala. 1970).

procedures. By 1978, out of 232 state troopers at the rank of corporal or above, none was black.[42]

Faced with a court order to develop a promotion test that did not adversely impact blacks, the department administered a test to 262 applicants, 60 of whom were black. Of these, only five blacks finished in the top half of the test-takers, and the highest rank achieved by a black candidate was 80. Under federal guidelines, tests are presumed to adversely impact blacks if they do not do at least four-fifths as well as whites.[43] In other words, as explained by the Court, "[I]f 60% of the whites who take a promotion test pass it, then 48 percent of the black troops to whom the test is administered must pass." Otherwise, the test is regarded as having an adverse impact on black job aspirants.[44] Under the unanimous 1971 Supreme Court holding in the *Duke Power Company* case,[45] an employer can justify administering a test with an adverse impact only on the basis of a compelling business need, a standard that opened a generation worth of litigation over the validity of tests administered by both public and private employers. Strangely, given the critical importance of a police force that appreciates priorities and procedures, knows and respects the law, and understands the importance of fastidious record keeping, the issue of a compelling state need to hire troopers who scored high on exams was not raised as an issue by either the majority or the dissenting *Paradise* justices.

By late 1983, there were only four black corporals but no sergeants, lieutenants, or captains. The district court ordered

---

42. *Paradise*, 480 U.S. at 159.
43. *Id.* at 160.
44. *Id.*
45. *Griggs v. Duke Power Company*, 401 U.S. 424 (1971).

that at least 50 percent of promotions to all ranks go to blacks, assuming they are qualified and the rank was less than 25 percent black. This plan would terminate when the 25 percent figure was reached or when the department came up with a promotion plan that had no adverse impact on blacks. As applied, the order appeared flexible, for example, in permitting all-white promotions when no qualified blacks were available. In fact, one upper-ranks promotion exam did produce a class with just over 23 percent blacks, a bit below the 25 percent goal.

A four-judge plurality, led by Justice Brennan, had little difficulty affirming "a temporary remedy that seeks to spend itself as promptly as it can by creating a climate in which objective, neutral employment criteria can successfully operate to select public employees solely on the basis of job-related merit."[46] As to any whites passed over by the remedial procedures, "[I]t cannot be gainsaid that white troopers promoted *since 1972* were the specific beneficiaries of *an official policy which systematically excluded all blacks*" (emphasis in opinion).[47] Concurring, Justice Stevens sensibly likened the case to the South's desegregation era, when busing and other race-conscious remedies were sometimes imposed in an effort to completely eliminate the legacy of forced separation of the races.[48]

Justices O'Connor and Powell both invoked the standard test for race-conscious official action—strict scrutiny to determine whether a compelling interest was being served by a narrowly tailored remedy. However, though Powell saw

46. *Paradise*, 480 U.S. at 156 (citing *NAACP v. Allen*, 493 F.2d 614, 621 (5th Cir. 1974)).

47. *Id.* at 170–171 (citing *Paradise v. Prescott*, 767 F.2d 1514, 1533 (11th Cir. 1985)).

48. *Id.* at 190–195.

nothing in Judge Johnson's handling of the matter to prevent his concurring with the plurality, Justice O'Connor was brief, but sharp, in her dissent, accusing her brethren of adopting "a standardless view of 'narrowly tailored' far less stringent than that required by strict scrutiny."[49] (More than a decade later, critics would make this same accusation regarding O'Connor's opinion in the Michigan cases.) The 25 percent requirement in *Paradise* was too rigid, she maintained. Instead, remedies such as stiff fines might have achieved the desired reforms "without trammeling on the rights of non-minority troopers," or a trustee might have been appointed to develop fair promotion procedures.[50]

One can, on the one hand, appreciate Justice O'Connor's desire to put some ground between her own developing affirmative action jurisprudence and the kind of result-oriented activism of such justices as Blackmun, Brennan, and Marshall. Her attempt, however, along with that of Justice Powell, to reduce each case to a pat formula—strict scrutiny, compelling need, narrow tailoring—is less convincing. There were, as we have seen, three distinct categories of affirmative action cases coming to the Court during this period: private contracts or consent decrees providing for racial preferences, state or federal initiatives designed to lift black people into the economic mainstream by awarding special benefits in areas like public contracting, and court-ordered remedies for specific acts of illegal discrimination. In the first category of cases, including *Weber*, the Court, instead of running roughshod over specific Civil Rights Act language, might instead have elected to "pierce the veil" of the transaction to determine whether it was in fact a remedy for past illegal discrim-

49. *Id.* at 197.
50. *Id.* at 200.

ination. If so, the parties, whether by agreement or consent decree, could well have been given some leeway to reach a just settlement. If not, the deal was itself barred by the Civil Rights Act of 1974 and should have been rejected.

The second category, including such cases as *Bakke* and *Fullilove* and involving no past official discrimination, presents the perfect situation for the "compelling need" standard. Strict scrutiny is appropriate; narrow tailoring, essential. The need for judicial skepticism is great because of the brutal and terrible history, both in this country and elsewhere, of the de jure use of race or ethnicity to define individual rights.

The third category, exemplified in such cases as *Sheet Metal Workers* and *Paradise* and involving judicial remedies for past illegal discrimination by public or private actors, calls for the application of a far different standard. Rather than strict scrutiny, judicial discretion should be the order of the day. Rather than narrow tailoring, the courts should be encouraged to think creatively for remedies that will purge the involved institution of the vestiges of its lawless conduct. Beneficiaries of the mitigating policies ought not to be limited to those suffering direct injury from the discrimination. In George Wallace's Alabama, for example, the operative policy for every institution controlled or influenced by the state— including the state troopers—could be summarized in three simple words: Blacks not welcome. Needed in this category is the complete dismantling of the system and its effects. To require blacks to go through the futile gesture of challenging the system in order to benefit from that dismantlement would compound the indignity.

In short, Justice O'Connor's "one size fits all" affirmative action analysis in those early years lacked subtlety and judicial imagination. However, her opinion in *Paradise* was joined by the new Chief Justice Rehnquist and the recently appointed Justice Scalia. Soon Justices Kennedy and Thomas would join the Court, and O'Connor's need to dissent in affirmative action cases would disappear.

Perhaps the most curious decision of the string that began with *Weber* involved not race but gender. In *Johnson v. Transportation Agency*,[51] a male county worker in Santa Clara County, California, had applied for the job of road dispatcher but lost the position to a woman judged slightly less qualified. The male worker alleged that his rights under Title VII of the Civil Rights Act had been breached. The Transportation Agency had recently adopted an affirmative action plan with the goal of making the ratio of male and female workers, as well as minorities in each department, reflect their proportion in the county labor force—36.4 percent female, for example. At the time, women constituted only 22.4 percent of agency employees and held none of the 238 skilled craft worker positions. Yet in trying Johnson's case, the district court found there had been no past or present discrimination practiced by the agency. Rather, as the agency itself reported, most women failed to undergo the training needed to compete for the jobs in question, many of the positions required heavy labor, and societal attitudes had tended to discourage women entrants.[52]

Ignoring the fact that as recently as *Wygant* it had held that societal discrimination is too amorphous a concept to justify race (or gender) conscious relief, a Court majority, again led by Justice Brennan, invoked the holding in the 1978 *Weber* case that employer action of giving hiring preference

---

51. *Johnson v. Transportation Agency*, 480 U.S. 616 (1987).
52. *Id.* at 625–627.

to minorities is justified to eliminate a "manifest imbalance in traditionally segregated job categories."[53]

Weber was profoundly different in one material respect— the employer in that case, Kaiser Aluminum, along with its craft unions, had been deeply involved in excluding minorities from the unions and apprenticeship programs that would have made those minorities eligible for skilled positions. Rather than engage in a costly and protracted legal battle, Kaiser chose to start a new chapter in its employment policies. By contrast, Santa Clara County had practiced no such discrimination.

Justice O'Connor, however, concurring with the judgment, chose to disregard the findings of the district court and to draw her own statistical conclusions from the evidence. The Court, she complained, "has chosen to follow an expansive and ill-defined approach to voluntary affirmative action by public employers despite the limitations imposed by the Constitution and the provisions of Title VII."[54] To introduce race-conscious hiring, an employer—public or private— must, in effect, acknowledge its own culpability for past discrimination. It must "point to a statistical disparity sufficient to support a prima facie claim under Title VII by the employee beneficiaries of the affirmative action plan of a pattern or practice claim of discrimination."[55] Once that is done, voluntary actions are encouraged as a remedy for past discrimination. In *Johnson*, in the total absence of female participation in certain job categories, Justice O'Connor found her prima facie case justifying a gender-conscious response. On the basis of the undisputed evidence—which

53. *Id.* at 633.
54. *Id.* at 648.
55. *Id.* at 649.

suggested no agency discrimination—Justice O'Connor appeared to be inventing facts to support her predetermined conclusion. There is simply no other basis on which to explain her decision.

Justice Scalia, in dissent, complained that the Court had transformed the Civil Rights Act, replacing "the goal of a discrimination-free society with the quite incompatible goal of proportionate representation by race and sex in the workplace."[56] This statement is true even if the action by employers "is intended to overcome the effect, not of the employer's own discrimination, but of societal attitudes that have limited the entry of certain races, or a particular sex, into certain jobs."[57]

Justice Scalia's analysis drew support from an unexpected source, Justice Stevens, who, in his concurrence, offered one of the more candid judicial statements one is likely to encounter—a flat admission that he (and the Brennan plurality group), in permitting race-conscious affirmative action, had baldly chosen to disregard the clear language of the Civil Rights Act. Without question, Justice Stevens acknowledged, the intention of Congress had been to preclude discrimination against or preferences for members of the majority or minority races. Years of observation, however, showed that "special programs to benefit members of minority groups" could speed the arrival of greater job equality, the true hope of those who supported the legislation. Neither the pre-*Weber* decisions of the Court, "nor the 'color blind' rhetoric used by the Senators and Congressmen who enacted the bill, is now controlling." So, for Justice Stevens: "[T]he only problem for me is whether to adhere to an authoritative con-

56. *Id.* at 658.
57. *Id.* at 666.

struction of the Act that is at odds with my understanding of the actual intent of the authors of the legislation. I conclude without hesitation that I must answer that question in the affirmative."[58] It would be hard to imagine a more bald statement of judicial activism than Justice Stevens' acknowledgment that his opinion was based on the silent aspirations of the legislators rather than the language of the bill or their publicly stated legislative intent.

The *Johnson* case brought to a close a period when employment cases were at the center of the Supreme Court affirmative action docket. The focus would next shift to government contracting, voting rights, and, of course, education. Pushed by such agencies as the EEOC and the Office of Federal Contract Compliance Review and sanctioned by the Court, industry was well into its affirmative action and diversity periods, seeking to employ minorities in numbers that at least reflected their participation in local labor forces. In the initial period, with the major exception of *Bakke*, most of the judicial focus was on the Civil Rights Act and little attention was paid to social questions raised by race preferences. The stigmatic effects of discrimination, for example, were so clear that few lawyers or justices stopped to wonder whether the promotion of less-qualified minorities or the admission of those with marginal academic credentials into the nation's elite universities would also raise questions of stigma. Beginning with the *Croson* case, however, it would fall to Justice O'Connor to address this and other questions for the Court majority.

---

58. *Id.* at 644.

Chapter Four

O'Connor in Command

Justice O'Connor stepped front and center as the leading judicial voice on affirmative action cases with her majority opinion in *City of Richmond v. J.A. Croson Company.* Jokingly described by one political observer as a city of "great social rest," the outwardly sleepy Virginia capital had also been capital of the Confederate States of America and a nerve center for the South's massive resistance to school desegregation in the 1950s. By the early 1980s, however, 50 percent of the population and five of the nine city council members were black. In 1983, the council passed an ordinance requiring that nonminority contractors subcontract at least 30 percent of municipal construction contracts to firms at least 51 percent owned and controlled by blacks, Hispanics, Asians, Native American Indians, Eskimos, or Aleuts. At the council meeting devoted solely to this matter, some of those present talked in general about discrimination in the construction industry and the difficulty that minority contractors had breaking into the business. Participants noted that only 0.67 percent of the city's prime construction contracts during the previous five years had been

awarded to minority firms. Although Richmond prevailed
against a challenge by a white contractor in the district court,
the Fourth Circuit Court of Appeals reversed,[1] noting the
Supreme Court's decision in *Wygant*, which had prevented
Jackson, Michigan, from laying off a white teacher while
maintaining a black with less seniority.

Justice O'Connor rejected the Richmond quota, with a
total of six justices coming down on the same side of that
issue. She dismissed the notion that the black share of Richmond's population—50 percent—was much of a starting
point for a finding of discrimination, insisting that the number of MBEs in the city would have better conveyed the uni-
verse from which contractors and subcontractors were
selected. Relying on "completely unrealistic" raw population figures betrays "an assumption that minorities will
choose a particular trade in lockstep proportion to their representation in the local population."[2] She also pointed out
that the record did not contain any direct evidence of discrimination on the part of the city or its prime contractors,
nor any evidence that the city knew the number of MBEs in
town or the percentage of work obtained by minority subcontractors. Without a showing of discrimination and with the
strict scrutiny the case required, Richmond could show neither a compelling need for its quota nor a narrowly tailored
remedy for addressing any need: "[A]n amorphous claim that
there has been past discrimination in a particular industry
cannot justify the use of an unyielding racial quota."[3] Further,
the seemingly random inclusion of other ethnic groups—"It
may well be that Richmond has never had an Eskimo or Aleut

1. *J.A. Croson Company v. City of Richmond*, 779 F.2d 181 (4th Cir. 1985).
2. *Croson*, 488 U.S. at 507.
3. *Id.* at 499.

citizen"—undermined rather than supported the city's claim that its quota responds to a pattern of discrimination.[4]

Lawyers for the city argued that with the Court having approved a 10 percent federal set-aside in *Fullilove*, "It would be a perversion of federalism to hold that the federal government has a compelling interest in remedying the effects of racial discrimination in its own public works program, but a city government does not."[5] O'Connor addressed this point unconvincingly, falling back on the special responsibility Congress has to implement the Fourteenth Amendment, which, along with the other Civil War amendments, "are limitations of the powers of the States and enlargements of the power of Congress."[6]

This clear constitutional mandate reinforced the need for strict scrutiny to "smoke out" illegitimate uses of race, a practice Justice O'Connor condemned in language stronger than any she had previously employed in affirmative action cases: "Classifications based on race carry a danger of stigmatic harm. Unless they are strictly reserved for remedial settings, they may in fact promote notions of racial inferiority and lead to a politics of racial hostility."[7]

Justice O'Connor's tone was strong and confident, and her recognition of the potential harm of race-conscious action was welcome. However, the decision did not convincingly distinguish itself from recent Court holdings to the contrary, and, in yielding to her developed tendency to narrowly apply her own edicts, the decision did away with far less state and

4. *Id.* at 506.
5. *Id.* at 489.
6. *Id.* at 490.
7. *Id.* at 493.

municipal race-conscious activity than was initially assumed.

For one thing, the federal-state explanation for approving a 10 percent set-aside in *Fullilove* while rejecting the 30 percent quota in *Croson* was inconsistent. True, Congress has a special responsibility to implement the Fourteenth Amendment, but it must do so in a constitutional manner affording due process to all races. The *Fullilove* evidence supporting congressional concern about difficulties faced by minority contractors was no more specific and, thus, in a constitutional sense, no more impressive than the evidence for *Croson*— testimony about difficulties minority contractors have with raising funds, posting construction bonds, and working up responsible bids. These obstacles purportedly explain the low number of minority bid winners. In *Fullilove*, the Court told the federal government to continue with its preferences, whereas in *Croson*, Justice O'Connor offered a handful of race-neutral steps that would make it easier for MBEs to compete at least for the smaller contracts. Clearly, as the Court balance shifted, Justice O'Connor and her brethren would seek opportunities to revisit this issue.

Justice O'Connor offered no explanation distinguishing her treatment of statistical information in *Croson* from that in *Johnson*. In both cases, the lower courts found no link between low minority or female participation in the activity in question and any official discrimination. Yet the miniscule percentage of successful minority bidders in *Croson* raised no problem for her, while the failure of females to seek heavy-duty road building work in *Johnson* established, in O'Connor's view, a prima facie case of discrimination by Santa Clara County. Why? The Court has often applied a lesser standard of scrutiny for gender-based distinctions, but that was not at issue here. Justice O'Connor offered no explanation for her contrary conclusions, and the passage of time has shed no new light on them.

Yet strikingly in *Croson*, Justice O'Connor remained open to the development of convincing evidence of discrimination, even providing a formula for its accomplishment: "There is no doubt that '[W]here gross statistical disparities can be shown, they alone in a proper case may constitute prima facie proof of a pattern or practice of discrimination.' . . . But where special qualifications are necessary, the relevant statistical pool for purposes of demonstrating discriminatory exclusion must be the number of minorities qualified to undertake the particular task."[8] With this succinct bit of guidance, Justice O'Connor transformed the denouement she appeared to have wanted—a lessening of reliance on race-conscious state contracting procedures to favor minority applicants—into a mad scramble on the part of hundreds of jurisdictions to find disparities sufficient to justify race-conscious relief. "Disparity studies" appeared in jurisdiction after jurisdiction, vouched for by a parade of expert witnesses translating low numbers of minority contracts into an inference of discrimination. Their claims were in turn disputed by other expert witnesses who saw in the same low numbers only a paucity of qualified minority bidders. Justice O'Connor had spoken forcefully about the evils of race-conscious decision making, but in terms of facts on the ground, her decision served mainly to educate jurisdictions on how best to insulate their race-conscious programs from successful challenge.

8. *Id.* at 501, 502.

A Lurch to the Left

The liberals on the Court were able to reassemble their affirmative action majority for the only time in the 1990s, in the case of *Metro Broadcasting, Inc. v. FCC.*[9] They used their fleeting power to rewrite judicial standards for considering race-conscious government action, only to have the new standards disowned after Justice Marshall surrendered his place on the bench to the conservative Justice Thomas. In view of the brevity with which it served as precedent, *Metro Broadcasting* is most noteworthy for the opportunity it presented Justice O'Connor to spell out in dissent a more complete version of the views she had articulated in *Croson.*

Metro Broadcasting involved a challenge to two rules promulgated by the Federal Communications Commission and designed to increase minority ownership of broadcast outlets. In 1986, minorities owned only 2.1 percent of the more than 1,100 radio and television stations in the United States.[10] The FCC suggested that increasing minority ownership would provide all citizens with a more diverse menu of viewpoints, present minorities depicted on radio and television in less stereotypical ways, and increase the employment of minorities by the broadcast industry. To help effectuate such change, the commission decided to treat minority ownership as one positive factor among several considerations in deciding among competing applicants for broadcasting rights. In addition, the commission made it easier for a licensee whose qualifications for holding a broadcast license had been placed under FCC review to unload the property through a "distress sale" to an FCC-designated

9. *Metro Broadcasting, Inc. v. FCC*, 497 U.S. 547 (1990).
10. *Id.* at 553.

minority. In fiscal year 1988, Congress endorsed this policy by including in its appropriation for the FCC a condition that no appropriated money be spent examining or changing its minority policies.[11]

In a dramatic departure from at least a half century of precedent, the Court, led by Justice Brennan, offered a relaxed standard by which the Court would judge benign race-conscious legislation: "We hold that benign race-conscious measures mandated by Congress—even if those measures are not 'remedial' in the sense of being designed to compensate victims of past governmental or societal discrimination—are constitutionally permissible to the extent that they serve important governmental objectives within the power of Congress and are substantially related to the achievement of those objectives."[12] No special scrutiny. No compelling governmental need. No narrow tailoring. No need for any past discrimination to be alleged. No limitation of relief to victims of alleged discrimination. No need to address the lingering effects of past discrimination. As long as a court considered the race-conscious behavior "benign"—presumably meaning it favored minorities at the expense of whites— and as long as it didn't take a court full of clerks to discern the relationship between some important governmental interest and the act in question, the Court would provide its blessing.

All the dissenters, Justices Rehnquist, Kennedy, and Scalia, joined Justice O'Connor's long, comprehensive dissent: "At the heart of the Constitution's guarantees of equal protection lies the simple command that the Government must treat citizens 'as individuals,' not simply as components of a

11. *Id.* at 560.
12. *Id.* at 564–565.

racial, religious, sexual or national class."[13] With *Metro Broadcasting*, the Court abandoned the safeguards of strict scrutiny, compelling need, narrow tailoring—long established to protect this concept. The reason for such scrutiny was to eliminate the division of the nation into racial blocs, thus escalating racial hostility and perhaps stigmatizing the minority. Congressional approval of preferences unlinked to specific past discrimination, though earning respectful consideration, should not alter the Court's responsibility or the standards of close scrutiny. The *Fullilove* decision, which approved the 10 percent set-aside for MBEs, was distinguishable because it was exercised by Congress under its special authority to implement the Fourteenth Amendment—it was part of congressional efforts to remedy past discrimination and never embraced the relaxed standard approved by the Court in *Metro Broadcasting*.

Particularly troubling, Justice O'Connor continued, was the majority's reliance on benign racial classifications: "'Benign racial classification' is a contradiction in terms. Governmental distinctions among citizens based on race or ethnicity, even in the rare circumstances permitted by our cases, exact costs and carry with them substantial dangers. To the person denied an opportunity or right based on race, the classification is hardly benign."[14] Further, the term "benign" conveys a sense of transient fashion rather than immutable principle: "Untethered to narrowly confined remedial notions, 'benign' . . . reflects only acceptance of the current generation's conclusion that a politically acceptable

13. *Id.* at 602.
14. *Id.* at 609.

burden, imposed on particular citizens on the basis of race, is reasonable."[15]

Then came a paragraph that would later haunt Justice O'Connor as she sought to explain her acceptance of the diversity-inspired race preference admissions procedures at the University of Michigan School of Law: "Under the appropriate standard, strict scrutiny, only a compelling interest may support the Government's use of racial classifications. Modern equal protection doctrine has recognized only one such interest: remedying the effects of racial discrimination. The interest in increasing the diversity of broadcast viewpoints is clearly not a compelling interest. It is simply too amorphous, too insubstantial, and too unrelated to any legitimate basis for employing racial classifications."[16]

O'Connor elaborated that such classifications should be reserved for remedial settings; they should not be invoked for "insubstantial" interests like program diversity: "This endorsement trivializes the constitutional command to guard against such discrimination and has loosed a potentially far-reaching principle disturbingly at odds with our traditional equal protection doctrine. . . . Like the vague assertion of societal discrimination, a claim of insufficiently diverse broadcasting viewpoints might be used to justify equally unconstrained racial preferences, linked to nothing other than proportional representation of various races."[17] Moreover, the concept of equating race with point of view rests on stereotyping and cannot be defended as narrowly tailored. That premise, according to the dissent, "is utterly irrational

15. *Id.* at 610.
16. *Id.* at 612.
17. *Id.* at 614.

and repugnant to the principles of a free and democratic society."[18]

Still, Justice O'Connor could not evade some reference to *Bakke*, in which Justice Powell had accepted some race consciousness in the interest of a diverse student body. This concept is true enough, acknowledged Justice O'Connor, but "only if race were one of many aspects of background sought and considered relevant to achieving a diverse student body."[19]

Finally, Justice O'Connor complained that the FCC had explored no race-neutral ways to achieve diverse viewpoints, including simply requiring more balanced and targeted material.[20]

With *Metro Broadcasting*, two well-defined visions of the standard by which affirmative action cases should be judged were grappling for supremacy on the Court. In the Brennan-Marshall view, benign government classifications were entitled to only enough court review to determine whether they reflected an important governmental interest and were substantially related to the achievement of that interest.

In the other view, race-conscious policies required strict scrutiny—judicial oversight—to ensure they served a compelling government interest, most often (if not exclusively) to redress specific past wrongs. Justice O'Connor had become the most articulate judicial advocate for this latter point of view, and, owing to her opinion in *Croson*, her view was the law with respect to state actions. *Metro Broadcasting*, however, bestowed only an intermediate standard of scrutiny upon federal actions. This decision could perhaps be justified

18. *Id.* at 618.
19. *Id.* at 621.
20. *Id.* at 622.

by distinguishing between the strict standard established for the states under the Fourteenth Amendment's equal protection clause, coupled with Congress' historic mandate to enforce the amendment against the states, and the standard established for the federal government under the due process clause of the Fifth Amendment.

In terms of stare decisis, *Metro Broadcasting* would enjoy the short adventurous life of a jackrabbit testing greyhounds. By the time the next federal program reached the Court, the liberal Justice Marshall had retired, replaced by the conservative Clarence Thomas, and Justices White and Brennan—who had both voted with the majority in *Metro Broadcasting*—had also left the bench, replaced by liberal Clinton Justices Ginsburg and Breyer, both considered likely to back intermediate review. The net conservative gain of one was enough to tip the balance on the Court.

All of that, however, did not occur until 1995, five years after *Metro Broadcasting.* During the interim, Justice O'Connor had the opportunity to discuss race-conscious decision making in the related field of redistricting. Following the 1990 census, North Carolina became entitled to a twelfth congressional seat. The legislature created one majority black district, but the U.S. attorney general refused to "preclear" the plan, claiming under the Voting Rights Act[21] that the state, with a black population of 20 percent, could have created a second majority black district. To gain clearance, the legislature engaged in a bit of gerrymandering, fabricating a district that was 160 miles long and that darted out from the farm country, through business and manufacturing centers along I-85 to gobble up every black enclave to the point where critics joked that a car driving along the interstate

21. *Voting Rights Act,* 42 U.S.C. 1971, 1973-1973p (2000).

with its doors open could kill most of the voters in the district.[22] The gerrymander did not disenfranchise whites or lessen their political influence. In fact, some voting analysts concluded at the time that concentrating black voters—who tend to vote overwhelmingly Democratic—in a handful of districts actually diluted Democratic voting strength in other competitive districts, costing the party congressional seats. Those initiating the suit, however, claimed they were being denied their Fourteenth Amendment right to participate in a color-blind election. The majority opinion in *Shaw v. Reno*, written by Justice O'Connor, and her actions in later related cases are noteworthy. First was the vehemence with which she expressed her abhorrence at the very notion of classifications of citizens on basis of race, borrowing from an earlier Supreme Court decision that said such classifications "are by their very nature odious to a free people whose institutions are founded upon the doctrine of equality."[23] Regarding racial gerrymandering, she had this to say: "A reapportionment plan that includes in one district individuals who belong to the same race, but who are otherwise widely separated by geographical and political boundaries, and who may have little in common with one another but the color of their skin, bears an uncomfortable resemblance to political apartheid."[24] The case was remanded for consideration of the evidence as to what, if anything, had been considered apart from race.

When read carefully, however, particularly in light of her subsequent decisions, it is clear that Justice O'Connor had no

22. *Shaw v. Reno*, 509 U.S. 630 (1993) (citing WASHINGTON POST, Apr. 20, 1993, at A4).

23. *Id.* at 643.

24. *Id.* at 647.

problem with race being one factor in redistricting, as long as more traditional considerations—geographic compactness, continuity, and respect for political subdivisions— were not given short shrift. According to O'Connor, race-conscious redistricting is not always impermissible. What is objectionable "is redistricting legislation that is so extremely irregular on its face that it rationally can be viewed only as an effort to segregate the races for purposes of voting, without regard for traditional districting principles and without sufficiently compelling justification."[25]

Concurring in the 1995 Georgia redistricting case, *Miller v. Johnson*,[26] which also involved the extreme application of race consciousness, Justice O'Connor found it necessary to assuage the concern of districts all across the nation, many of which reflected at least some race consciousness. "Application of the Court's standard does not throw into doubt the vast majority of the Nation's 435 congressional districts, where presumably the States have drawn the boundaries in accordance with their customary districting principles. That is so even though race may well have been considered in the redistricting process."[27]

This statement is vintage O'Connor. First, state your argument in the most powerful fashion, and then narrow the applicability of your decision to the specific facts at hand, providing yourself with the maximum flexibility to decide the next case in a seemingly different way. This is a good formula for maintaining strategic influence on the Court, even if it does carry a price among those who feel important shared principles have been abandoned.

25. *Id.* at 642.
26. *Miller v. Johnson*, 515 U.S. 900 (1995).
27. *Id.* at 928.

The case that proved the vehicle for reversing *Metro Broadcasting—Adarand Constructors, Inc. v. Pena*[28]—involved a fairly typical provision in a federal contract entitling the prime contractor to a bonus should he hire subcontractors owned and controlled by socially and economically disadvantaged individuals, normally a euphemism for preferred minorities. Adarand, the low bidder on a federal highway guardrail subcontract, brought suit after losing the bid to a firm owned by a preferred minority. Adarand lost at the district and appellate court levels when both courts applied the *Metro Broadcasting* "substantially related" standard to the transaction.[29] However, Justice O'Connor, backed by Chief Justice Rehnquist and Justices Kennedy, Thomas, and Scalia, dismembered *Metro Broadcasting* and left even *Fullilove*, which had approved an earlier government-mandated set-aside program, quaking.

O'Connor said that prior to *Metro Broadcasting*, the Court had been evolving to embrace three clear principles: skepticism (strict scrutiny) toward any preference based on racial or ethnic criteria; consistency in applying the law to anyone burdened or benefited by the racial or ethnic classification; and congruence, a coming together of the equal protection and due process clauses of the Fourteenth and Fifth Amendments.[30] According to Justice O'Connor, the three principles undermined by *Metro Broadcasting* "all derive from the basic principle that the Fifth and Fourteenth Amendments to the Constitution protect persons, not groups."[31] Government actions based on race employ a group classification recog-

---

28. *Adarand Constructors, Inc. v. Pena*, 515 U.S. 200 (1995).
29. *Id.* at 210.
30. *Id.* at 223–224.
31. *Id.* at 227.

nized in most situations as "irrelevant and therefore prohibited. . . . Accordingly, we hold today that all racial
classifications, imposed by whatever federal, state, or local
governmental actor, must be analyzed by a reviewing court
under strict scrutiny. In other words, such classifications are
constitutional only if they are narrowly tailored measures
that further compelling governmental interests."[32]

Typically, O'Connor also sought to assure civil rights
advocates that there was still room for the government to
operate, disclaiming any notion that strict scrutiny is "strict
in theory, but fatal in fact." Instead, a successful effort had to
focus on amelioration of wrongs: "The unhappy persistence
of both the practice and the lingering effects of racial discrimination against minority groups in this country is an unfortunate reality, and government is not disqualified from acting
in response to it."[33]

Concurring, Justice Thomas found a succinct way to
describe his thinking: "Government cannot make us equal; it
can only recognize, respect and protect us as equal before the
law."[34]

32. *Id.*
33. *Id.* at 237.
34. *Id.* at 240.

Chapter
Five

The
Percentage
Plans

In 1995, Texas found its race pref-
erence programs in higher education struck down by the federal appellate court. The following year, Proposition 209, a
California ballot initiative, banned such preferences in education and state employment and contracting. Then Florida
Governor Jeb Bush's "One Florida" executive order decreed
policies similar to California's. In each state, education officials responded with one version or another of what came to
be known as "percentage plans." These plans were guarantees that high school students graduating in the top reaches
of their respective classes—4 percent in California, 10 percent in Texas, and 20 percent in Florida—would find places
in the state university system. Like officials everywhere,
political and educational leaders in the three percentage plan
states had their eyes on the University of Michigan, where a
confrontation involving that school's race preference programs was gathering steam. Not only might their own programs be affected by the result, but their experiences
operating in what were legally preference-free regimes would

likely be inspected closely by the interested parties in the Michigan case.

The state of Florida was the only state in the nation to file an amicus brief against the University of Michigan race preference programs. Apart from an abstract interest in affirmative action law, the state's apparent purpose for using the brief was to trumpet the "One Florida" alternative—also known as the "Talented 20 Plan"—implemented by Governor Jeb Bush.[1] Bush moved not under the lash of court edict but rather under the threat posed by Ward Connerly, the California Board of Regents race preference foe who was still riding high after his 1996 Proposition 209 victory that abolished race preferences in state employment, contracting, or college or university admissions.[2] (Prop 209 is discussed in more detail later in this chapter.) Connerly had come to Florida promising to enact a similar referendum. Bush, who regarded Connerly's presence as incendiary, was also facing a legal challenge to Florida's race-conscious programs. To blunt both, Bush came forward in October 1999 with his own version of the ban on race preferences, implemented by executive order.

In terms of higher education, the plan guaranteed admission into the state's higher-education system, which consisted of eleven universities, to any student graduating in the top 20 percent of his or her high school class.[3] (This guarantee was not to any particular school in the system.) A more restrictive threshold of 10 or 15 percent was rejected by the governor's advisors because that number would not yield

1. Brief for the State of Florida as Amicus Curiae Supporting Petitioner, *Grutter v. Bollinger*, 123 S. Ct. 2325 (2003) (No. 02-241).

2. *See* Cal Ed Code § 87100 (2003).

3. Brief for the State of Florida, at 8–10.

enough minorities. "Florida has provided alternative but race-neutral means of admission to those students who are striving for excellence, but who may have been disadvantaged by a lack of educational opportunities," reads the brief. "Respect for the principle of nondiscrimination need not come at the expense of maintaining racially and ethnically diverse institutions of higher learning."[4] Connerly's effort was defeated by a decision of the Florida Supreme Court, which held that his ballot initiative failed to meet the clarity standards of the state's constitution.[5]

In Texas, the percentage plan was spurred by the 1996 ruling of the Fifth Circuit Court of Appeals in the *Hopwood*[6] case, which held that all race preferences in university admissions were in violation of the Fourteenth Amendment's equal protection clause. The court concluded that in the famous *Bakke* case, Justice Powell, in permitting race to be used as a plus factor for diversity purposes, had written only for himself. The Supreme Court had long since moved beyond Powell's "lonely opinion."[7] More recent Court decisions made it clear that race is no more rational "than would be decisions based upon the physical size or blood types of applicants."[8] The laws in Texas, Louisiana, and Arkansas, the three states over which the Fifth Circuit presided, followed suit. The University of Texas Law School at Austin had invited so sweeping a ruling by baldly maintaining what had been separately maintained, color-coded applicant files for whites and minorities, with different presumptively admit, presumptively reject, and discretionary files all

---

4. *Id.* at 2.
5. *Id.*
6. *Hopwood v. Texas*, 78 F.3d 932 (5th Cir. 2000).
7. *Id.* at 945.
8. *Id.*

pegged to something very close to admissions quotas for whites, blacks, and Hispanic Americans.[9] In addition to lowered academic admissions standards, the school also maintained segregated waiting lists. In 1992, the year Hopwood and her fellow plaintiffs applied to the law school at Austin, 55 Hispanics and 41 blacks were among the 514 students admitted. Without race preferences, the corresponding numbers would have been 18 and 9.[10] In response to the decision, a group of Democratic state legislators drafted a bill guaranteeing qualified applicants admission to any of the thirty-five state universities of their choice. The universities were permitted, under the legislation, to extend the option to the top 25 percent within each high school and to consider any of eighteen other factors in determining admissions policies.[11] Governor George W. Bush signed into law the measure, which had no purpose other than maintaining minority admissions at levels as close to the pre-*Hopwood* days as could be achieved by "race-neutral" means.

In California, Proposition 209, also known as the California Civil Rights Initiative, was adopted by voters in November 1996. In anticipation of its passage, the Board of Regents had the previous year voted to abolish the consideration of race or ethnicity in admission to the state's nine research universities and twenty-three regional universities, beginning with the 1997–98 academic year.[12] Under a plan adopted in 1960, the top 12.5 percent of high-school graduates had

9. *Id.* at 936.
10. Id at 937.
11. Sylvia Moreno, *House OKs Measures on Admissions*, DALLAS MORNING NEWS, Apr. 16, 1997, at A17.
12. Catherine L. Horn & Stella M. Flores, *Percent Plans in College Admissions: Comparative Analysis of Three States' Experiences* (available at www.civilrights project.harvard.edu) (2003).

been guaranteed admission to one of the nine research schools, and the top 35 percent had qualified for regional or specialty schools. In the heyday of affirmative action, the flagship schools in the system went to extraordinary lengths to maintain the desired mix of black and Hispanic students. In 1998, for example, the combined SAT scores of blacks at Berkeley, most of whom had been admitted before the ban on preferences, were 288 points below those of whites.[13] Early in his first term, Governor Gray Davis introduced legislation guaranteeing the top 4 percent of each high school graduating class admission to one of the research universities comprising the University of California. The plan was in short order approved by the Board of Regents and became known as Eligibility in Local Context (ELC). Davis also proposed putting more weight on SAT 2 scores, which measure proficiency in three subjects of the student's choice, as opposed to SAT 1, which tends to measure more abstract intellectual abilities and which is regarded by educators as a far more reliable indication of a student's college potential.[14] Richard Atkinson, president of the University of California, threatened to scrap the SAT 1 test altogether, again despite its documented value in predicting first-year grades, the likelihood of completing undergraduate school, and the probability of pursuing graduate studies.[15] Atkinson's threat brought results as the Educational Testing Service (ETS) promised to at least review its product for hidden bias. Like Florida, but unlike Texas, California universities require

13. Yvonne Daley, *Berkeley Recruits Minorities*, BOSTON GLOBE, May 2, 1999, at A12.

14. Michelle DeArmond, *California Governor Proposes 4 Percent Solution*, ASSOCIATED PRESS, Jan. 5, 1999.

15. John Leo, *An Unfair Ticket to College*, U.S. NEWS AND WORLD REPORT, Feb. 18, 2002, at 59.

from their high school students a number of specific academic courses in such subjects as English, math, science, and
foreign language. All three programs demand that SAT or
ACT scores be submitted, though technically those scores do
not count toward qualification.

Before examining the specifics of implementation of the
percentage plans, it would be useful to note a few of their
generic qualities. First, as a matter of principle, the plans may
or may not meet the Fourteenth Amendment problem that
critics of affirmative action had with previous admissions
policies. Standing alone, a simple ELC-type plan could probably pass muster. Adorned with enough legislative jewelry
to make sure this "race neutral" approach produces the
appropriate racial results, however, the effort may begin to
resemble the assortment of "freedom of choice," or pupil
assignment, schemes used by the South to thwart integration
two generations ago.

Second, in terms of education, depending on the design
of the plans, they may abort the very result that many opponents of race preferences thought would be quite useful—the
redistribution of minority beneficiaries of affirmative action
from the most elite schools, where many were guaranteed to
finish in the lower percentiles of their class, to lower first-tier
or higher second-tier schools where minorities' academic
credentials would make them highly competitive. Scholars
have debated whether affirmative action stigmatizes or per-
petuates negative stereotypes with respect to its intended
beneficiaries.[16] Whatever the case, elemental good sense suggests that a college applicant should, in most cases, be paired

16. *See* Andrew F. Falaby, *An Analysis of the Supreme Court's Reliance on
Racial Stigma as a Constitutional Concept in Affirmative Action Cases*, 2 MICH. J.
RACE & L. 235.

with an institution at which he or she will feel intellectually compatible.

Third, from the university's perspective, percentage plans replace an efficient way of selecting minority students with a terribly imprecise method. Forced to choose between acknowledged or concealed affirmative action plans, one suspects that most admissions officers would choose something akin to race-norming, whereby white students and minorities are considered separately but each on the basis of academic merit, as the term is traditionally employed. Percentage plans, on the other hand, unless modified, can easily result in students from failing secondary schools with unchallenging curricula qualifying for automatic admission, while far better prepared students who fall just below the cut-off are denied admission. In practice, this can mean substituting inner-city blacks from segregated academic environments for well-prepared middle- and upper-middle-class blacks—86 percent of the African Americans who attend elite universities fall in one of these latter two categories—from more integrated settings.[17]

Fourth, to achieve their barely concealed function of providing the substance of affirmative action without the name, the percentage plans depend on the continuing bank of virtually segregated secondary schools.

Fifth, the plans have no applicability to graduate schools.

Sixth, the plans work best with less-competitive universities, where a majority of the 4, 10, or 20 percenters would have gotten in anyway. This drives home the fact that the heart of the affirmative action debate has always been over the access of blacks and other minorities to elite schools. A

17. Justin Ewers, *A Glimpse of Life Without Affirmative Action*, U.S. NEWS AND WORLD REPORT, Mar. 31, 2003, at 48.

very large number of colleges and universities where fine educations can be obtained are far from highly selective in their admissions practices.

Seventh, the plans have no applicability to out-of-state students.

Finally (and fatally), by ignoring such standardized tests as the SAT and ACT, the plans purport to discard a highly predictive indicator of future academic success in such areas as grades, graduation rates, and the likelihood of continuing on to graduate school.

The initial impact of ending racial preferences was a decline of black and Hispanic applicants to the more selective California and Texas institutions and a far milder drop in Florida, even in the flagship schools—the University of Florida at Gainesville and Florida State University in Tallahassee. Black student applications to the University of Texas Law School fell by 42 percent; Hispanic applications, by 12 percent. In 1997, 10 black students were admitted to UT-Law for the fall semester, compared with 65 the previous year; 4 blacks and 26 Hispanics entered UT-Law as first-year students, compared with 31 blacks and 42 Hispanics in 1996, which was the last year of affirmative action. University-wide at Austin, black applications declined by 26 percent and those from Hispanics fell by 23 percent.[18]

California experienced the same sort of shock. In 1997, even before the ban on affirmative action was fully in place, undergraduate black applications to the University of California system dropped by 8 percent, while those from Hispanics fell 4 percent. Meanwhile, 17 percent fewer minority students were admitted to the graduate schools at UC-Berke-

18. Renee Sanchez, *Minority Admissions Fall with Preferences Ban*, WASHINGTON POST, May 19, 1997, at A1.

ley, and Boalt Hall Law School at UC-Berkeley admitted 80 percent fewer black students and 50 percent fewer Hispanics than it had a year earlier. Only a single African American student enrolled in that first-year Boalt Hall class. Other graduate programs also experienced a drop in minority candidates. The Haas Business School saw black student admissions drop 52 percent, and Hispanic admissions, 54 percent. In graduate engineering programs, Hispanic admissions dropped 43 percent, from 50 to 29, and black admissions dropped 18 percent, from 28 to 23.[19]

"I think those are shocking numbers," said Andrea Guerrero, a UC-Berkeley law student. "Berkeley has lost its place of pre-eminence and prominence by allowing this to happen."[20]

Jerome Karabel, long a force for race preferences at the University of California at Berkeley, called the anti-affirmative action trend "the biggest negative redistribution of educational opportunity in the history of the country."[21]

"The solution is to bring into the university admissions process a sufficient pool of black, Chicano and Latino high-school students from which we can draw, and not to label us bad guys for revealing the cancer in the K–12 system," said Bruce E. Cain, acting director of Berkeley's Institute of Governmental Studies.[22]

Scarcely noticed in the early cries of doom was the fact

19. Renee Koury, *Report Says 17 Percent Fewer Minority Students Admitted at California-Berkeley Graduate Schools*, SAN JOSE MERCURY NEWS, June 26, 1997, at B1.

20. *Id.*

21. James Traub, *The Class of Prop. 209*, NEW YORK TIMES MAGAZINE, May 2, 1999, at §6, 44.

22. Patrick Healy, *Berkeley Struggles to Stay Diverse in Post-Affirmative Action Era*, CHRONICLE OF HIGHER EDUCATION, May 29, 1998, at A31.

that minority enrollment at some of the less-competitive campuses—Riverside, Irvine, and Santa Cruz, for example—was
increasing, precisely the sort of "cascade" phenomenon critics of race-conscious admission policies had predicted. The
new reality was captured brilliantly by James Traub, a contributing writer to the *New York Times Magazine*, who found
black and Hispanic students productively working toward
graduation and advanced degrees without the unremitting
academic pressure that would have been their lot at one of
the state's two supercompetitive universities. "I think I am
more prepared in terms of graduate school than I would have
been had I gone to U.C.L.A.," volunteered one African American student. "Some of the professors there are not necessarily as humble as they are here."[23] Traub reported candidly
that the central problem in California was the underperfor-
mance of black elementary and secondary school students
relative to others. Some 30 percent of all Asians qualify for
the state university system, 12.7 percent of whites, 3.8 percent of Latinos, but only 2.8 percent of blacks—an appalling
547 during 1996.[24] In addition, few of the students Traub
interviewed thought diversity a small virtue to be discarded
in a fair contest with merit. Most saw it as a "piety" rather
than something real. "Most of the white and Asian students
I spoke to felt quite cut off from the black and Latino students.
Social life was largely Balkanized by ethnic identity. Only a
few classes were small enough for the kind of sustained discussion that would feature the black or Latino 'view.' And
the number of minorities in such upper level classes was very
small."[25] Ward Connerly saw the distribution or cascading of

23. Traub, *The Class of Prop. 209*, at 44.
24. *Id.*
25. *Id.*

minority students to the less-selective state universities as a positive thing. "I'm extremely heartened by the numbers," he said. "Minority students are saying 'I'm disappointed I didn't get into Berkeley, but I proved I can get into Riverside or Santa Cruz on my own.' It means one has to wonder how these kids got onto campus."[26]

However, the University of California quickly tailored its procedures to the perceived need to reach minorities without using formal race-conscious policies. UC-Berkeley, for example, adopted strategies such as the following: high school GPA weighted by the academic quality of courses taken, scores on required standardized test, participation in academic-enrichment programs, additional evidence of intellectual or creative achievement, extracurricular activities, leadership and other personal qualities, and likely contribution to the intellectual and cultural vitality of the campus, perhaps a code term for contribution to diversity. The school also paid attention to "personal struggle" and "difficult personal and family situations or circumstances." Similar considerations have since been appropriated by the UC graduate schools. UCLA Law School, for example, came up with an affirmative action plan for low-income students that includes assessing the poverty of the applicant's neighborhood and the accumulated wealth of the applicant—two criteria concentrated among black and Latino candidates. The school also gave special consideration to students agreeing to major in critical race theory, a radical legal ideology that states such doctrines as equal protection are disguised tools of racism.

However, even with all the crafty non-race-conscious ways to restore the racial balance of the mid-1990s, the situation, from the university's point of view, is mixed. The per-

26. *Id.*

centage of blacks in the university system is still below the affirmative action years, but the percentage of admitted Hispanics is up a bit. Both are down if measured by first-year enrollees—Hispanics from 13.8 percent in 1996 to 13.5 percent in 2001; blacks from 3.8 to 3.0 percent in the same two years.[27] Things are even tighter at the two flagship schools. In 1996, 6.5 percent of enrolled first-year students at UC-Berkeley were black, as were 6.3 percent of the same class at UCLA. The corresponding figures for Hispanics were 15.7 percent at UC-Berkeley and 19.0 percent at UCLA. In 2001, the numbers were 3.9 percent blacks at UC-Berkeley and 3.4 percent at UCLA. The Hispanic numbers were 10.8 percent at UC-Berkeley and 14.4 percent at UCLA. At Boalt Hall, in 2002, Hispanics held 13 percent of the first-year places, up 2.4 percent from 1996. Blacks remained well below their 1996 number of 7.6 percent. Perhaps most tellingly, in the fall of 2003, Boalt Hall, with its "holistic" admissions gimmicks, succeeded in enrolling fourteen black students in its first-year law class. However, nine of those black students averaged nine points below entering white first-year law students, which is identical to the average gap during the affirmative action years.[28] At the core of black underrepresentation lies the real problem, black underachievement.

Some of the early Texas reaction to the *Hopwood*-induced drop in minority representation at flagship schools bordered on panic. "There is no way I can go on competing successfully in drawing qualified minorities if things continue this way," predicted Dean Michael Sharlot, of the University of Texas

---

27. Horn & Flores, *Percent Plans in College Admissions*, at 55.
28. *Id.*

Law School.[29] Critics of *Hopwood* feared that the black law students who were forced to go elsewhere to seek education would not return to Texas to practice. Dallas Mayor Ron Kirk, an African American graduate of the law school at Austin, warned, "The way you have judges who are people of color ten years from now is to have graduates coming out of the law school now."[30] On the other hand, such less-selective schools in the Texas system as Prairie View, Houston, and Texas Tech saw minority applications increase substantially. A note contrary to Mayor Kirk's was sounded by Edward Blum, the Texan who headed the Campaign for Color Blind America. Blum maintained that weeding out those who are less qualified academically is no disservice to education. At schools like Rice, he noted, the SAT gap was a hefty 271 points, but more than 25 percent of the blacks dropped out compared with just over 10 percent of the whites. (At Berkeley, the SAT gap was 288 points, and the respective dropout rates were 42 percent for blacks and 16 percent for whites.) Blum further noted that more than half the blacks who graduated from the University of Texas Law School flunked the bar exam on their first try, and a high percentage of those failed it the second time as well. "UT's pass rate on the exam was lower than Baylor's," he claimed, "owing to affirmative action."[31]

Saying all that, however, in seven years the UT system witnessed a 15 percent increase in African American stu-

29. Lydia Lum, *Applications by Minorities Down Sharply*, Houston Chronicle, Apr. 8, 1997, at 1.

30. Jayne Noble Suhler, *1 Black Set to Enroll So Far As New Law Student at UT; Dean Blames Ban on Race-Based Admissions*, Dallas Morning News, May 21, 1997, at A1.

31. Edward Blum, *Hopwood May Raise Minority Graduation Rates*, Dallas Morning News, Dec. 14, 1997, at J6.

dents and a 10 percent jump in Hispanics.[32] Taken as a whole, the thirty-five institutions of higher learning became more regionally diverse, increasing the representation of rural areas and inner cities. Top 10 percenters were doing as well at the University of Texas as their non–top 10 percent peers. "Believe me," declared Bruce Walker, director of admissions at UT-Austin, "every day of the week, I wake up wishing I could have affirmative action back. But this is the dish we got served and we're making the best of it."[33]

As Walker's words imply, Texas essentially defined "making the best of it" by attempting to bring the percentage of minority enrollment back to pre-*Hopwood* levels using means that were technically non-race-conscious and thus at least arguably within the law. In 1997, the first post-*Hopwood* year, UT-Austin revamped its admission policy to include not only the traditional academic index, but also a personal achievement index (PAI), consisting of leadership, scores on two essays, extracurricular activities, awards and honors, work experience, service to school or community, and "special circumstances." This latter category included the socio-economic status of the family, whether the student came from a single-parent home, the language spoken at home, the applicant's family responsibilities, socioeconomic status of the school attended, and the average SAT/ACT scores of the school attended relative to the applicant's own scores. Although many of these PAI items can be used as proxies for race, the political mandate from Austin was to restore the pre-*Hopwood* racial balance, the fruits of a system to which most faculty and administration had been deeply committed

32. *Id.*

33. Kenneth J. Cooper, *Colleges Testing New Diversity Initiatives*, WASHINGTON POST, Apr. 2, 2000, at A4.

but which now had—temporarily at least—become illegal. In the fifth in its series of reports on the Implementation and Results of the Texas Automatic Admissions Law, released in fall 2002, UT-Austin cited approvingly the call by University of California System President Richard Atkinson for this "holistic approach," including his call for reducing the emphasis on test scores. The approach had succeeded in restoring most of the pre-*Hopwood* racial balances, though total black enrollment was still 7 percent below 1996 levels. Students admitted under the 10 percent program maintained slightly higher SATs than those admitted through regular procedures—1226 versus 1222.[34] African American representation continued to experience problems at the graduate level, which was beyond the reach of the top 10 plan. For example, although the representation of Hispanic Americans at UT-Law had returned to pre-*Hopwood* levels, the percentage of African American law students had dwindled from 6.4 percent to 3.6 percent of the entering class. Black representation was also down sharply in other graduate programs, including medicine. By 2003, throughout the entire Texas system, the number of blacks had increased about 15 percent since *Hopwood*, and the number of Latinos was up to about 10 percent. Overall at UT-Austin, however, black enrollment was down 17 percent since *Hopwood*, and Latino enrollment was down 5 percent. At Texas A&M, black enrollment was down 14 percent, and Latino enrollment, 1 percent.[35] For Texas to do even this well it took hard work, including proac-

34. Gary M. Lavergne & Bruce Walker, *Academic Performance of Top 10% and Non-Top 10% Students: Academic Years 1996–2001* (available at www.utexas.edu/student/research/reports/admissions/HB588-Report5.pdf).

35. Mitchell Landsberg, Peter Y. Hong, & Rebecca Trouson, *Race-Neutral University Admissions in Spotlight*, LOS ANGELES TIMES, Jan. 17, 2003, at Metro 1.

tive recruiting in new areas, aggressive distribution of schol-arships, and establishment of academic relationships in parts of the state and individual towns that had previously drawn few minority applicants. Such programs do little to inform the preference debate because they are not unique to per-centage plans, they are supported enthusiastically by both supporters and opponents of race preferences (one possible exception being race-conscious scholarship awards), and they will no doubt become an even more important tool for colleges and universities regardless of future changes in the law of affirmative action.

The Florida Plan

In its brief opposing the University of Michigan race prefer-ences, the state of Florida declared that in One Florida, it had found a "better" way: "Florida's plan is better in that it no longer accepts the lack of quality in the public schools that serve our underprivileged children; better because it recog-nizes the need to provide mentoring, tutoring, and other extra attention to those underprivileged children and their teach-ers; better because it encourages all students regardless of race or economic status to aspire to post-secondary educa-tion; better because it no longer accepts a separate standard on the basis of race; better because it focuses on providing all races with the opportunity to meet common standards; and finally, [better] because it looks forward to a day when racial classifications and separate standards are no longer deemed necessary by anyone."[36]

This soaring rhetoric amounts to something of an unsup-portable boast for a system that, at the time the brief was

36. Brief for the State of Florida, at 19.

submitted, had been in full operation for fewer than three years. To the contrary, the record to date could better support the following statements about One Florida:

1. The plan is an inherently poor test of the efficacy of race-neutral college admission systems, because applying a very tolerant top 20 eligibility requirement on a system where the two most selective state universities already admit more than 60 percent of all applicants is a bit like testing a foul shooter's accuracy by having him toss basketballs into a lake. An estimated 99 percent of students admitted under the Talented 20 Plan would have been admitted even had no such plan been in existence.

2. Many of the programs Florida maintains to make its system work, such as mentoring high-school students and encouraging greater numbers of students to take the PSAT, are not truly alternatives to affirmative action. Rather they are useful efforts to improve the academic performance of high-school students—something that would be worth trying regardless of the college admissions system involved.

3. A handful of the programs that are designed to sweeten the mix of college applicants with greater numbers of minorities are themselves race preference programs vulnerable to legal challenge.

4. Certain adjustments in the state's admissions standards are thinly veiled substitutes for race preferences and would be vulnerable to the extent that the initial program was.

The Talented 20 Plan casts a wide but porous net. Of the 11,539 who enrolled at state universities, fewer than 200 had maintained high-school GPAs of 3.00, traditionally the minimum requirement for admission to the state system. Another 10,933 did not enroll at state schools. The change in minority numbers throughout the system was negligible, with the exception of the state's most selective school, the University of Florida at Gainesville, where the average SAT score is just short of a lofty 1300 and where the percentage of black first-year students fell from 11.8 to 7.2 percent, and the number of Latinos from 12 to 11 percent in 2001, the first year of One Florida's operation.[37] University of Florida Provost David Colburn said, "The minority students that we can accept are also being recruited by Harvard, Princeton and the University of California."[38]

University officials acknowledged the black presence would have been even more modest had the school not revised its admissions criteria. The *St. Petersburg Times* reported that under the new standards, "A high SAT score, for example, now counts no more toward admission at UF than two years of attendance at a high school in a low income neighborhood."[39] Membership in the National Honor Society counted less than having grown up in a high-crime neighborhood. It could not have surprised many when black enrollment surged during the second year of the program's operation. With something of a flair for understatement, the *Los Angeles Times* reported, "In fact although the policies are legally race-neutral, the explicit goals are to achieve ethnic and racial diversity."[40]

Opponents of traditional race preferences find themselves divided over the question of race-neutral alternatives

---

37. Barry Klein, *Black UF Freshman Numbers Plummet*, St. Petersburg Times, Aug. 12, 2001, at A1.

38. *Id.*

39. *Id.*

40. Brief for the State of Florida, at 19.

designed to achieve the same ethnically balanced end. Roger Clegg, of the Center for Equal Opportunity, argued, "I don't think any institution—a legislature or a bowling club—has to have a particular ethnic or racial mix."[41] On the other hand, Terrence Pell, a senior counsel at the Center for Individual Rights, which led the legal battle against Michigan, considered diversity a legitimate goal as long as the right means are used to achieve it. "Schools ought to be free to experiment with a variety of strategies that serve their educational purposes and missions," he told the *Washington Post*. "The Michigan legislature has the right to expect that the University of Michigan serves the residents of Michigan, all residents of Michigan. It's a public university."[42] In California, Tom Wood, the father of Prop. 209, and Ward Connerly, its most prominent advocate, also split on the issue. Had *Grutter v. Bollinger* gone the other way, it is not at all clear that affirmative action opponents would have been able to maintain a united front in opposition to the norms of evasion that would quickly have spread across the nation's campuses.

Although most race consciousness in the percentage plan states is disguised, One Florida continues an overt program designed to spur black interest in and eligibility for the state university system. UF-Gainesville and others offer specific scholarships to minority students that are not available to whites. Governor Jeb Bush sought and received a steep increase in funding for the College Reach-Out Program (CROP), which identifies promising minority students and helps them prepare for college through tutors, "homework clubs," and in-school academic strategy sessions. CROP has also established a partnership with the college board to

41. Cooper, *Colleges Testing New Diversity Initiatives*, at A4.
42. *Id.*

increase minority participation in advanced placement (AP) courses, PSAT testing, and SAT preparation. The administration has also paid a great deal of attention to student performance on the Florida Comprehensive Assessment Test (FCAT), which records performance in a variety of subjects in grades 3–10, and has backed both public and private alternatives to so-called failing schools. As effective as these measures may be, however—and whether or not they are race conscious—they all have their roots in the affirmative action era, and all, or most, would have continued in one form or another regardless of how the Michigan decision came down. The core of the percentage plans involves seeking to maintain or restore diversity where race preferences have been done away with. On the incomplete evidence to date, California, Texas, and Florida offer little to cheer about.

Doctoring Economic Affirmative Action

In March 2003, Anthony P. Carnevale and Stephen J. Rose published a Century Foundation Paper titled *Socioeconomic Status, Race/Ethnicity, and Selective College Admissions*, which used data from two longitudinal studies published by the National Center for Education Statistics to make the case for affirmative action programs that pay primary attention to the applicant's socioeconomic status (SES)—a figure that combines family income with the education and occupation of the parents. They found that the underrepresentation of low SES students at 146 of the "most selective" four-year institutions—defined by the Barron's Guide—was far more severe than the underrepresentation of blacks and Latinos. For example, blacks and Latinos, representing 15 and 13 percent of the college-age population, respectively, each had about 6 percent of the entering class. By contrast, 74 percent of the students at the top 146 colleges came from families in the top SES quarter, whereas 10 percent came from the bottom half of the SES scale, and only 3 percent from the bottom quartile.[43] There are four times as many black and Hispanic students as there are students from the lowest SES quartile. In fact, with colleges busy admitting legatees, football players, and favored racial and ethnic groups, those in the lower reaches of SES fare worse than would be the case if GPAs and standardized test scores—the traditional determinants of merit—were the sole considerations of admissions offices.[44]

Apart from conceptual unfairness, the current state of affairs strikes a blow against social and economic mobility. It is well documented that, all other things being equal, going to a top-tier school enhances one's chances of graduating and attending graduate school. Most studies also suggest that top-tier attendance carries at least a modest advantage in terms of future income.

In their advocacy of race preferences, *The Shape of the River*, authors William Bowen and Derek Bok argued, "The problem is not that poor but qualified candidates go undiscovered, but that there are simply too few of these candidates in the first place."[45] Carnevale and Rose argue, however, that "[t]here are large numbers of students from families with a low income and low levels of parental education who are academically prepared for bachelor's degree attainment, even in the most selective colleges."[46] Richard Kahlenberg,

43. Anthony P. Carnevale & Stephen J. Rose, *Socioeconomic Status, Race/Ethnicity, and Selective College Admissions*, at 11 (available at www.equaleducation.org) (March 2003).

44. *Id.*

45. Ethan Bronner, *Study Strongly Supports Affirmative Action in Admissions to Elite Colleges*, NEW YORK TIMES, Sept. 9, 1998, at B10.

46. Carnevale & Rose, *Socioeconomic Status*, at 38.

of the Century Foundation, who endorses affirmative action on the basis of income rather than race, noted, "Only 44 percent of low SES students who score in the top quartile academically attend a four year college."[47] Carnevale and Rose refer to this group as "low hanging fruit" for selective schools.[48] Kahlenberg also cited research by Donald Heller, of Pennsylvania State University, who suggested that many prestige schools could increase their commitment to educating SES-disadvantaged students. For example, Pell Grant recipients, who generally come from the bottom 40 percent SES, make up 32 percent of the student body at UC-Berkeley and 24 percent at Smith, but only 7 percent at Princeton and Harvard.[49]

Critics of affirmative action pegged to economic status maintain that the plans fall into one of two categories: those that would benefit whites or Asian Americans—say children of recently divorced or unemployed parents or recently arrived immigrants, or those that are thinly disguised race preference programs. Not only are there more poor whites than blacks in absolute terms, but even the lowest-income whites tend to score higher on standardized tests than do blacks of any strata.[50] With some tweaking, however, the beneficiary configuration can change. Carnevale and Rose noted that although blacks average 12 percent of the students at those schools diligently practicing affirmative action and would constitute only 4 percent at selective schools where academic merit alone was the standard, they would bounce back to 10 percent under the current SES standard, which

47. Richard Kahlenberg, *Economic Affirmative Action in College Admissions*, at 4 (available at www.tcf.org).
48. Carnevale & Rose, *Socioeconomic Status*, at 39.
49. Kahlenberg, *Economic Affirmative Action*, at 6.
50. *Id.* at 42.

includes family income, education, and occupation.[51] Add accumulated wealth and quality of the neighborhood, or even single parenthood, and schools would be able to maintain minority representation at current levels, or even above, albeit with many of the current core of economically comfortable blacks replaced by those from less-privileged backgrounds. (For reasons not evident from their scholarship, the authors recommended keeping a separate race-conscious affirmative action program in place.) Carnevale and Rose urged that qualifying SAT scores be kept in the 1000–1100 area, about where they are for current affirmative action beneficiaries. They cited data indicating that students who attend the tier-one schools and who had SAT scores in the 1000–1100 range graduate at an 86 percent rate.[52]

There is little doubt that low-SES students are being penalized by race-conscious affirmative action. Not only are some of their potential places taken by blacks and Latinos, but also the dollars expended on affirmative action are dollars not available to assist low-income students. It is also quite clear that many among the nation's leading institutions of higher learning attach low priority to the recruitment or admission of low-SES individuals. It would seem, however, that by the time the low-SES plan authors get through tweaking economic affirmative action programs to wring out any possibility that preferred minorities will suffer a net loss, we once again will have a disguised race-conscious program. Whether the beneficiaries are white, black, or polka dot, by reaching down to the 1000–1100 SAT level at our most prestigious colleges, we would be perpetuating the annual crea-

51. *Id.*
52. *Id.* at 34.

tion of an academic underclass of students destined for the
low percentiles of achievement.

Underlying the notion of economic affirmative action, as
with that of racial affirmative action, is the sense that the
nation's social and economic classes should remain fluid,
open to newcomers, and rich with plausible examples of
upward mobility in this society. As long as access is based
on merit, this is the role public and even private colleges and
universities have played and will continue to play. Over the
years, we have watched one immigrant group after another
arrive as wretched masses yearning to breathe free. All experienced poverty, all felt the sting of discrimination, some felt
the violence of the nativist, the demagogue, the rabble rouser.
All—Irish, Italian, Jew, Pole, and others—eventually thrived,
their communities lifted by the assimilation made possible
by quality elementary and secondary school education. University education came later, earned by the diligence of the
newcomers, the guidance of their elders, and the commitment of society to provide opportunity for those deserving of
it. In more recent years, Filipinos, Chinese, Vietnamese, and
other Asians followed suit, with traditionally good results.
One expects that Hispanics, the latest group to arrive in massive numbers, will participate in a similar upward mobility
through education with or without affirmative action.

However, our colleges are institutions of learning, not
social alchemy. The problem is that there are simply not
enough competent African American students to work with.
Deprived as a race of the immigrant experience, subjected to
enslavement, abuse, and scorn beyond the imagination of the
others, many of the younger generation resist the broad cultural assimilation that was at the root of all others' success.
For this condition, there is guilt enough to share, but the issue
is not guilt, it is sound policy. The nation must choose

between one policy set that offers equal opportunity on a playing field as fair as our society can make it and a second that offers entitlement by color, reward by race, preference through gimmick and contrivance. If too few students low on the SES scale are attending the most selective colleges, the likely solution involves identifying those with potential early in their K–12 experience and providing them with the educational resources to maximize their talent. If blacks and Hispanics are underrepresented at the elite institutions, the same applies—intervene early enough and effectively enough to provide real options for those involved. Affirmative action that begins as race preferences in college admissions is a testament to a failed policy, not the road map to a successful one.

Chapter Six

The Michigan Case

On August 2, 1996, the *Detroit News* ran a short piece on the third page of its Metro section, reporting that a group of professors was trying to find out whether state colleges and universities were applying the same admissions standards to applicants regardless of race or ethnicity. The group, the Michigan Association of Scholars, was affiliated with the National Association of Scholars and, like the parent organization, had been waging an offensive against the movement for political correctness in such areas as speech codes, racial preferences, and other manifestations of the diversity mantra. Its ultimate target was the University of Michigan at Ann Arbor, simply because, despite its 60 percent undergraduate admissions rate, it was by far the most selective university in the state and maintained a number of graduate programs, like its law school, that were even more selective in picking students. The national data on minority performance on standardized tests suggested that few would be admitted to the university without substantial preferences.

Few of the state schools that the association surveyed

rushed forward with the requested information, despite the fact that at several, admissions standards were so relaxed as to border on open enrollment. For its part, the University of Michigan appeared more anxious to provide rhetoric than numbers. "What we're doing comports with the law and is appropriate," said Lisa Baker, a public affairs officer. "The best evidence of success is that we have one of the highest retention rates in the country. Around 94 to 95 percent of freshmen go on to become sophomores. Over 85 percent of all students graduate in six years. For African Americans, the rate is 70 percent, one of the highest in the country."[1]

However, procedures begun under the state's Freedom of Information Act and the intervention of four Republican state legislators opposed to race preferences soon pried the numbers loose. On June 22, 1997, the *News* published a front-page report based on a computer analysis of the statistics that the paper had acquired from the school showing that blacks, Hispanics, and Native Americans were admitted to the University of Michigan at dramatically higher rates than Caucasian and Asian students with the same grades and test scores. In 1995, for example, 78.6 percent of the so-called underrepresented minorities (African Americans, Hispanics, and Native Americans) who applied to the undergraduate program were admitted, whereas the figure for nonminorities was 69.4 percent. That same year, underrepresented minorities with a B average and SAT scores of 1000–1090 were admitted at a rate of 93.4 percent, but only 19.5 percent of whites and Asians with the same qualifications were admitted. With that same B average and a 22 or 23 ACT score, 93.7 percent of blacks and Hispanics, but only 12.7 percent of

---

1. Rusty Hoover, *College Admissions Officials Confused by Recent Rulings on Race*, DETROIT NEWS, Aug. 12, 1996, at C1.

whites, were admitted. With a GPA in the 3.0–3.24 range and LSAT scores ranging from 161 to 163, none of the nine Asian applicants and only two of forty-two whites were admitted, but 100 percent of the ten Hispanic Americans or blacks were admitted."[2]

The system used a grid that weighted such factors as race, history of overcoming discrimination, and economic status heavily enough to more than compensate many black and Hispanic applicants for substantially lower GPA and SAT credentials. With no apparent shame, the university publicly maintained a facade of equal treatment. For 1995, the official university catalogue declared: "[T]he University of Michigan is committed to a policy of nondiscrimination and equal opportunity for all persons regardless of race, sex, color, religion, creed, national origin or ancestry . . . in employment, educational programs and activities, and admissions."

Before long, the four legislators, David Jaye, Deborah Whyman, Gregg Kaza, and Michelle McManus, had generated legislative hearings on the University of Michigan admissions practices and were informally searching for rejected white or Asian American students willing to entertain a lawsuit. The Washington-based Center for Individual Rights (CIR), recent victors in the *Hopwood* case, decided to test not only Michigan's undergraduate admissions program but also the less formulaic but no less discriminatory law school procedure, which each year sought to achieve a "critical mass" of preferred minority students. For plaintiffs against the undergraduate program, CIR selected Jennifer Gratz and Patrick Hammacher. Gratz, a high-school cheerleader and homecoming queen who graduated fifteenth in

2. *Race and Reconciliation: What's Fair? U-M Policy Gives Minorities an Edge*, DETROIT NEWS, June 22, 1997, at A1.

her high-school class, would become the first in her family to graduate college. After being rejected by the University of Michigan-Ann Arbor, she gave up her ambition to become a doctor and enrolled at UM-Dearborn, a commuter school. As her lawsuit made its way toward the Supreme Court, Gratz graduated, got married, and went to work as a project manager and software trainer for a West Coast–based supply chain management company. "I didn't realize just how differently they treat people based on skin color until I filed the lawsuit," Gratz told the *Detroit News.*[3]

Patrick Hammacher, a white man from the predominantly black city of Flint, was recruited as Gratz' co-plaintiff. A graduate of Luke Powers Catholic High, he was wait-listed and then rejected by the University of Michigan, despite a hefty 28 on his ACT exam. He enrolled at Michigan State— which then and now accepts at least 85 percent of its applicants and thus needs no affirmative action program, graduated with a degree in public administration, and went to work as an accountant for Flint's Department of Recreation.

To challenge the law school program, CIR selected Barbara Grutter, a 47-year-old mother of teenage sons who ran a health care consultant business from her home. The daughter of a minister, Grutter had attended high school in Canada and believed she offered the law school both the diversity it advertised and the likelihood of success it sought. Despite a GPA of 3.8 at Michigan State and an LSAT score of 161, placing her in the eighty-sixth percentile, Grutter was rejected. Her academic credentials would have meant automatic acceptance for preferred minorities. In addition to feeling the lash of discrimination, Grutter took her rejection as

3. Jodi S. Cohen, *Three Lives Converge at the U.S. Supreme Court,* DETROIT NEWS, Mar. 24, 2003.

an affront to common sense, telling the *Detroit News*, "I had an application where I had demonstrated success in multiple fields. There's no question about whether I would be successful."[4]

The Long Minority Quest

The University of Michigan had dabbled with the race issue during the 1960s but had never found an academically sound way of dramatically increasing the presence of black students on campus. In 1970, a crisis forced its hand as the Black Action Movement (BAM), formed during the black power heyday of the late 1960s, threatened to shut down the campus unless its "demands" were met. As recounted by University President Robben W. Fleming, those demands included "enrolling 10 percent of the total student body from black applicants, thereby equaling the proportion of blacks in Michigan's population; recruitment of more black faculty and administrators; financial aid for black students to attend the university; further development of the Afro-American studies program; a center at which black students could congregate; and a few lesser items."[5] At the time, black enrollment was 3.5 percent. A study commissioned by Fleming concluded that with an intensive effort the percentage could be doubled within a reasonable time. The problem in going beyond that point, then as now, was that there were too few qualified blacks. Lowering the university's threshold would have meant ensuring black students' place at the bottom of the academic totem pole, perhaps to have many of them fail— "a sad end to an academic career that might have succeeded

4. *Id.*
5. ROBBEN W. FLEMING, TEMPESTS INTO RAINBOWS 207 (1996).

in a less competitive milieu."[6] Also, taking unqualified blacks would have meant penalizing whites who otherwise would have been accepted.

As BAM strike threats intensified, Fleming and his team produced a "compromise," which included a *goal* of 10 percent black students by 1973–74; tinkering with admission criteria in such a way so "that increased enrollment may be achieved *while at the same time preserving the satisfactory probability of successful completion of the educational program at the university*"; the devotion of additional funds to support enrolled blacks; recruitment of additional black faculty and staff; continuing the development of the Afro-American studies program; and development of a black students' center.[7]

BAM soon rejected the offer because the 10 percent goal was not a firm commitment, and it launched a strike under the slogan "Open It Up or Shut It Down." In response, 500 faculty members placed full-page ads in a number of regional newspapers saying, "It is time for voices to be raised against the actions of the few who are driving the university community into chaos."[8] During the next several days, however, supporters of the BAM strike stormed buildings and disrupted classes, broke furniture, threw books off library shelves, and released ammonia and stink bombs in several buildings.[9]

The strike was finally settled with BAM abandoning its demand for a guaranteed 10 percent of the class in favor of the university's aspirational approach. Looking back on the

6. *Id.* at 210–211.
7. *Id.* at 212.
8. *Id.* at 212–213.
9. *Id.* at 214.

episode a quarter-century later, Fleming said he would change little of what he did. Serious violence had been avoided, "we established much-needed programs for the advancement of black people,"[10] and the university remained in the forefront of the nation's institutions of higher learning. Yet the university also took the first major steps toward a selective lowering of academic standards, instituted racial targets, and put in place policies that would increase rather than decrease social and academic segregation. In addition, in treating the BAM demands as fit subjects for negotiation— particularly in an environment of coercion if not terror—the university, as one professor expressed to Fleming, was admitting "explicitly or implicitly that we are indeed a repressive, racist institution—but that is still a lie."[11] Editorially, the *Detroit News* seemed to summarize matters quite well: "When a great university, guilty only of excessive tolerance, goes begging on its knees for the forgiveness of arrogant radicals it's time for someone with authority and guts to step in and call a halt to the farce."[12]

Fleming made a brief, unfortunate encore as acting university president in the late 1980s after his successor, Harold Shapiro, abandoned Ann Arbor for the presidency of Princeton. Shapiro had been unable to make good on the university's commitment to boost black admissions to near 10 percent. Meanwhile, a number of racial incidents—including racial slurs directed against black students—brought a new round of BAM demonstrations and a campus visit by Jesse Jackson. Jackson engineered new commitments from Shapiro, who then left for the quieter confines of New Jersey.

10. *Id.* at 219.
11. *Id.* at 216.
12. *Id.* at 217.

Having structured a university where race influenced admissions, curriculum, living, and social facilities, Fleming and his entourage of the 1980s sought to mitigate some of the inconvenient consequences of that policy by regulating speech. With the apparent participation of several law school professors and at least the theoretical blessing of law school dean Lee Bollinger—who opined that, consistent with the First Amendment, there was much speech the university could regulate—they imposed a Policy on Discrimination and Discriminatory Harassment of Students in the University Environment. The policy prohibited students, under threat of sanctions, from "stigmatizing or victimizing" individuals or groups on the basis of race, ethnicity, age, marital status, handicap, or Vietnam-era veteran status. A guidebook, known as the Yellow Booklet, attempted to sharpen the vague prohibitions of the policy through specific example. For instance: "A male student makes remarks in class like 'Women just aren't as good in this field as men,' thus creating a hostile learning atmosphere for female classmates." Other stated offenses included telling jokes about gay men or lesbians, displaying a Confederate flag on the door of your room, or two men demanding "that their roommate in the residence hall move out and be tested for AIDS."

Thus, the code provided a basis for prosecuting a student who expressed the widely shared scientific view that various types of learning abilities and emotions are sex-linked. The new code was used to prosecute a dental student who repeated something a friend had told him about minorities having difficulty with a particular second-year dental course. Another student was prosecuted for expressing the opinion that homosexuality was a disorder that could be treated by counseling, and a young male who slipped a joke under a female's door suggesting that mopping floors was a female task was prosecuted. As noted by Jeff Jacoby in the *Boston Globe*, the code seemed calculated to prove the indictment of historian Alan Kors and civil liberties advocate Harvey Silvergate who, in *The Shadow University*, said that lively campus discourse "has been replaced by censorship, indoctrination, intimidation, official group identity and 'group-think.'"[13] Like the "closet doves" of the Johnson administration, Bollinger—who also banned military recruiters from the law school because of their ban on gays and lesbians—would later cast himself as an inside opponent of the policy. Until what would prove a successful legal challenge found its way into federal courts, however, this scholarly champion of First Amendment rights was little more than an ornament for campus tyranny. Ultimately U.S. District Court Judge Avern Cohn threw out the code as unconstitutional.[14]

Soon afterward, the university chose a new president, James Duderstadt, a former engineering school dean and, at 6 feet, four inches, a physically imposing visionary who took the cause of diversity and turned it into a managerial cult. America, he felt, was in the process of becoming a majority minority nation where whites would no longer predominate. The university must help prepare for that day, not only by reshaping its curriculum or redoubling efforts to attract diverse groups to the campus, but also by turning itself into an engine of pervasive change. Minority faculty were to be hired whenever "targets of opportunity" appeared.[15] Need and merit scholarships were to be heavily weighted toward minorities in a way one administrator called "disproportion-

13. Jeff Jacoby, *A Harvard Candidate's Silence on Free Speech*, BOSTON GLOBE, Mar. 1, 2002, at A15.

14. *John Doe v. University of Michigan*, 721 F. Supp. 852 (E.D. Mich. 1989).

15. FREDERICK R. LYNCH, THE DIVERSITY MACHINE 281–285 (1997).

ate by design.''[16] The school would undertake a vast expansion of minority recruitment. An office of minority affairs was to be created. The school would identify and support faculty, student, and staff "change agents." Multicultural education was to be enhanced. Affirmative action records were to become part of the evaluation criteria for department chairs, deans, and administrators.

Duderstadt called his creation the Michigan Mandate. Administrators hopped on board, urging all to follow the president's lead, seeking to undermine what one described as a culture that was "white-male and task oriented,"[17] with the sort of values another listed as "science-oriented, research oriented, competitive (striving to be the best in everything), elite and 'supercompetent' oriented."[18] In the words of Frederick R. Lynch, whose fine book, *The Diversity Machine*, devotes an entire chapter to the Michigan Mandate: "The Mandate and its top-down implementation reek of a high-level hubris that social change can be planned and even micromanaged."[19] Lynch noted that the Mandate left no room for such bedrock concepts of Western culture as "equality of opportunity, freedom of speech or association, capitalism, due process, individualism and individual rights, equal protection of the laws, the U.S. Constitution and universal standards or truths."[20] Lynch described an incident involving a course taught by senior sociology professor David Goldberg. In a session devoted to regression analysis, Goldberg sought to illustrate how such variables as education, age, class, and marital status could reduce *broad* apparent disparities in the

16. *Id.* at 288.
17. *Id.*
18. *Id.*
19. *Id.* at 282.
20. *Id.* at 314.

earnings of men and women, thus undermining the simplistic male exploitation models many of the students had carried into the classroom. Radical students not even in the course filed a formal grievance against Goldberg, charging him with racial and sexual harassment. While the specific complaints were dismissed as unsubstantiated, Goldberg's department chair did remove him from teaching all required courses.[21]

By the mid-1990s, the Mandate, in its cruder forms, was running out of steam. The Gingrich Revolution—itself less an augur of profound change than it seemed at the time— brought to power a Republican Congress less sympathetic to political correctness and the type of social innovation making its run on campuses like Michigan. The *Hopwood* case cast a long shadow over race preference policies in university admissions, as did the decision by the California Board of Regents to end such preferences, a decision soon underlined by California's electorate in passing Proposition 209. The conservative student publication, *Michigan Review*, regularly critiqued the Mandate, a battle many carried on even after graduation. Jeff Muir, a former *Review* staff writer, complained that the university had been admitting blacks and Hispanics who were poorly qualified to compete and that this was reflected in poor academic performance and lower graduation rates. Muir charged that Duderstadt's program had been at least partly responsible for a drop in Michigan's selectivity ranking by *U.S. News and World Report* and a drop in the university's overall ranking to the mid-twenties.[22]

Still, the university and its constituents pressed on. "We've admitted we're a racist institution," affirmative

21. *Id.* at 298.
22. *Id.* at 299.

action officer Zaida Giraldo told Lynch. "Minorities have sought a comfort level in self-segregation, and now we're working on curriculum reform."[23] Asked by the *Chronicle of Higher Education* how his school would respond to a *Hopwood*-style lawsuit, Duderstadt replied, "We will continue to do this until the Supreme Court says we can't any more. . . . If certain avenues are shut off, we'll try to find other ways to get the same results."[24] By the time the university and law school suits were filed in October and December 1997, respectively, however, Duderstadt had retired and the task of mounting a defense fell to his successor, the former law school dean Lee Bollinger.

Bollinger appreciated from the outset that the case would probably come down to the fluid vote of a single justice and that Sandra Day O'Connor had time and again invited a showing of evidence to justify affirmative action sufficient to meet the strict scrutiny standard imposed in such cases. Michigan could not permit itself to walk into a judicial haymaker as Texas had done. Instead, it must mobilize the business, professional, and educational communities nationwide who would bear witness to society's compelling need for blacks and other minorities trained at the nation's elite institutions. Moreover, it would not be enough for Justice Powell's diversity formulation to survive; it had to be brought down to the specifics of the University of Michigan, which must prove the educational benefits of diversity at this specific institution. This was where affirmative action would make its stand. No expense would be spared.

The legal team was potent, including its two principal in-house players, Jonathan Alger and Evan Caminker. Alger was

23. *Id.* at 301.
24. *Id.* at 309.

hired from the American Association of University Professors, where he had been working on an amicus brief for the university. Before that, he had been deputy civil rights counsel in the U.S. Department of Education. As deputy counsel, Alger would marshal and direct amicus support and get all relevant communities on record. Caminker, dean-elect of the law school, worked mainly on preparing theories and arguments for the law school brief. In charge of the *Gratz* case would be John Payton, a brilliant veteran civil rights lawyer, who was at that time a partner in the powerful Washington firm, Wilmer, Cutler and Pickering. Maureen Mahoney, a former clerk to Chief Justice Rehnquist and now a partner in the Washington firm of Latham and Watkins, was also a veteran Supreme Court advocate with a very good batting average; she would argue *Grutter.*

In the end, fighting the case cost the university an estimated $10 million.[25] By contrast, the university's prime adversary, the Center for Individual Rights, tapped Kirk O. Kolbo, a partner with the Minneapolis firm of Maslon Edelman Borman & Brand, but a novice in both civil rights and Supreme Court advocacy. Kolbo agreed to serve for expenses only. CIR's costs reportedly totaled about $4 million.[26]

Responsibility for providing Michigan with the evidentiary base that Bollinger thought necessary went to Professor Patricia Y. Gurin, chair of the Psychology Department. Gurin offered a report undergirding her expert testimony on the positive effects of campus racial and ethnic diversity on learning outcomes. However, she had one threshold problem:

25. Jodi Cohen, *Road to Supreme Court*, DETROIT NEWS, June 16, 2003, at B16.

26. 2002–2003 Annual Report of the Center for Individual Rights (available at www.cir-usa.org). *See* Janet Miller, *U-M Suit Cost Already $9 Million*, ANN ARBOR NEWS, Mar. 21, 2003.

Her study was based on a subset of a massive undergraduate longitudinal database for the 1985–89 period for the Cooperative Institutional Research Program (CIRP), which offered virtually no support for her conclusion. Indeed, the CIRP study found no correlation between structural diversity—the percentage of minority students on campus—and such educational outcomes as student knowledge, completion of the course of study, or performance on such post-baccalaureate exams as the LSAT, the MCAT, and the GRE.[27] Instead, Gurin offered some very weak linkage between what she called "classroom diversity" and "citizenship engagement," which were measured four and then nine years later and the latter of which included such items as hours per week spent on volunteer work, importance of participating in a community action program, and associating or making close friends with people of a different race.

Gurin's report was critiqued both by Robert Lerner and Althea K. Nagai for the Center for Equal Opportunity and by Thomas E. Wood and Malcolm J. Sherman for the National Association of Scholars.[28] Apart from the central problem of a database that disconfirms her thesis, the two critiques noted that Gurin offered a small but statistically significant relationship between what she called "classroom diversity" and so-called diversity activities, such as socializing with someone of a different race or ethnicity. Gurin's "classroom diversity" simply involved taking a course such as African American studies, something that might be done even if there were no blacks on campus. At no point did she report the

27. Expert Witness Report of Patricia Y. Gurin (available at www.umich.edu/~urel/admissions/legal/expert/gurintoc.html).
28. Lerner & Nagai, *A Critique of the Expert Report of Patricia Gurin*; Wood & Sherman, *Race and Higher Education.*

relationship between structural diversity and these positive behavioral outcomes. Further, as Lerner and Nagai noted, "Items for the four-year and then for the nine-year surveys under citizenship engagement appear to be proxies for political liberalism. There are no questions that discuss political activism that manifests a conservative tendency (e.g., attending an anti-abortion rally, the importance to you of reducing federal taxes, reducing government regulation, importance of participating in a free speech movement, attending a Second Amendment rally, or bringing a property rights case, etc.)."[29] Lerner and Nagai also inconveniently recalled that the initial study noted that the college experience "tends to make blacks more activist than when they enter, and divides the races politically, which is exacerbated by their tendency to segregate themselves."[30]

An even more devastating critique was later offered by Judge Danny Boggs of the Sixth Circuit in his powerful dissent from the appellate court's 6-5 en banc decision: "The Gurin Report is questionable science, was created expressly for litigation, and its conclusions do not even support the Law School's case."[31] For one thing, Gurin's report took no position on how much diversity is needed for benefits to kick in or increase. Moreover, it based its benefit claims on the softest data imaginable, "subjective self-reports of students and . . . low response rates to boot."[32] Also, the report did not even purport to measure any statistical link between the benefits it claimed and a more diverse student body. One small but statistically significant correlation it does provide—

29. Lerner & Nagai, at 17.
30. *Id.* at 39.
31. *Grutter v. Bollinger*, 288 F.3d 803 (6th Cir. 2002).
32. *Id.* at 804.

between taking such "classroom diversity" courses as African American history and good academic outcomes—is not related in any way to the number of minority students on campus. Why did Gurin develop proxy categories instead of the real thing? The reason for this bizarre methodology, which neither Gurin nor any other self-respecting academic would have offered as, say, a doctoral thesis, was clear to Judge Boggs: "I fear that Gurin used the proxies because a study of mere student body diversity either did not or would not produce the results that she sought."[33]

Tactically, however, the Gurin Report was a master stroke, finding its way with approval into the opinions of U.S. District Court judge Patrick J. Duggan, the Sixth Circuit majority, and Sandra Day O'Connor.

By the time of the lawsuits, both admissions processes had gone through considerable evolution. Understandably, with some 13,000 applications to consider, as opposed to some 5,000 law school applicants, the Literature, Science, and Arts (LSA) undergraduate process involved less individualistic consideration of applicants and was thus more formulaic. In 1995 and 1996, LSA used a set of grids with GPA ranges depicted on the vertical axis and ACT/SAT scores on the horizontal axis. According to Judge Duggan, "In 1995 four grids were used: (1) in-state non-minority applicants, (2) out-of-state non-minority applicants, (3) in-state minority applicants, and (4) out-of-state minority applicants. In 1996 only two grids were used: (1) in-state and legacy applicants and (2) out-of-state applicants with non-minority applicant action codes listed in the top row of the grid's cells, and minority action codes listed in the bottom row. In 1997, the same grids as in 1996 were used. However, in 1997, the LSA

33. *Id.*

also added .5 to underrepresented minority applicants' GPA scores."[34] Stunningly, the plan included the one thing specifically ruled unconstitutional in *Bakke*, a quota. Because the class was selected on a rolling basis instead of at one fixed time, a certain number of seats were designated for such favored groups as minority candidates, athletes, and in-state students. In response to a written interrogatory, the university explained that "[t]his space is 'protected' to enable OAU [Office of University Admissions] to achieve the enrollment targets of the University and of the individual units while using a rolling admissions system."[35] If insufficient numbers of the racially preferred were found, the protected seats could go to wait-listed or other applicants; theoretically, that could have happened at UC-Davis as well. The LSA grid system precluded consideration of whites in certain of the lower indices, but no preferred minority was ever excluded from consideration automatically.

In 1998, the LSA, apparently aware that it was headed toward legal defeat, implemented its 150-point procedure, which was in effect at the time the case reached the Supreme Court. This system awarded up to 80 points for a perfect GPA and 20 points for minority status, but only 12 points for a perfect SAT/ACT score and only 3 points for a brilliant application essay.[36] Although university officials would testify during pretrial deposition proceedings that the new procedures "change only the mechanics, not the substance" of its previous practice, Judge Duggan would, on December 13, 2000, hold the discarded procedures unconstitutional even though the new ones passed muster. Duggan found that "a

34. *Grutter v. Bollinger*, 137 F. Supp. 2d 821 (E.D. Mich. 2001) at 826.
35. *Gratz v. Bollinger*, 122 F. Supp 2d 811 (E.D. Mich. 2000) at 831.
36. *Id.*

racially and ethnically diverse student body produces significant educational benefits such that diversity, in the context of higher education, constitutes a compelling governmental interest under strict scrutiny."[37] He reached this conclusion, as would the appellate and Supreme Courts, despite the utter absence of credible evidence linking racial diversity to positive educational outcomes. Judge Duggan also found the LSA system was narrowly tailored in that it provided for the competitive consideration of race consistent with Justice Powell's *Bakke* mandate. He found this despite the fact that the new procedures still produced so great an advantage for minorities that anyone in the preferred category considered "qualified" for the university—that is, someone who was a good bet not to flunk out—would nearly always win acceptance.

The law school race preference policy, which eventually would win Supreme Court approval, had its genesis in the 1960s with the nearly complete failure of minorities to gain admission through race-neutral means. In 1966, the admissions committee began giving special attention to "those who are Negroes or from disadvantaged backgrounds," and those who had made the waiting list were given preference. In 1970, the admissions dean announced he would admit enough black and Hispanic applicants "who fall below admissions standards regularly applied" to comprise 10 percent of the class.[38] In subsequent years, the law school faculty debated the issue frequently, deciding that black and Hispanic students should constitute between 10 and 12 percent of each class, the beneficiary category later expanding to American Indians and Puerto Rican Americans.

---

37. *Id.* at 824.
38. *Grutter*, 137 F. Supp. 2d at 831.

Allan Stillwagon, who was Director of Admissions from 1979 to 1990, testified that he lacked the discretion to disregard the numerical targets,[39] which resulted in wide disparities among regular and special admittees. In 1988, for example, those regularly admitted had a median LSAT score of 43 and a median undergraduate grade point average (UGPA) of 3.58, while beneficiaries of race preferences had a median LSAT of 34 and a median UGPA of 3.05.[40] The 1989 Law School Announcement justified the preferences: "In administering its admissions policy, the Law School recognizes the racial imbalance now existing in the legal profession and the public interest in increasing the number of lawyers from the ethnic and cultural minorities significantly underrepresented in the profession. . . . Black, Chicano, Native Americans and many Puerto Rican applicants are automatically considered for a special admissions program designed to encourage and increase the enrollment of minorities."[41]

In 1992, a law school faculty admissions committee issued a Report and Recommendations that would become the governing policy to this day. The faculty dismissed the notion that LSAT results were meaningless, indicating that they accounted for an average of 27 percent of the difference in performance among students for three of the past four classes. Further, "as the size of the differences in applicant index scores increases, the value of the index as a predictor of graded law school performance increases as well." What conclusion should be drawn from these facts? "Bluntly, the higher one's index score, the greater should be one's chances

39. *Id.* at 830.
40. *Id.* at 826.
41. *Id.* at 829.

of being admitted. The lower the score, the greater the risk the candidate poses."[42]

Individual circumstances and characteristics may justify exceptions, but representatives of preferred races or ethnic groups should be considered despite low LSATs and UGPAs, because "this may help achieve that diversity which has the potential to enrich everyone's education and thus make a law school class stronger than the sum of its parts."[43] This statement represented no change in policy. For years, preferences were shown for blacks, Chicanos, Native Americans, and Puerto Ricans dwelling on the mainland. "By enrolling a 'critical mass' of minority students, we have ensured their ability to make unique contributions to the character of the Law School; the policies embodied in this document should ensure that those contributions continue in the future."[44]

The document is striking mainly in its transparent, albeit belated, attempt to reconcile existing practice with *Bakke*. Thus, whereas earlier policy statements made no mention of the academic joys of diversity, this one repeatedly sought to establish those benefits as a central objective. In addition, although an ad hoc *Bakke* majority held quotas unconstitutional, those same justices said nothing about "critical mass"—a notion more relevant to nuclear physics than law. In this case, the faculty tinkered with a concept that might provide the virtues of an outright quota system without the legal detriment. As one faculty member testified during the bench trial, "[W]e all understood the governing authority to be *Bakke*. . . . So I wanted the numbers out."[45] Yet, the law

42. *Id.*
43. *Id.* at 827.
44. *Id.*
45. Testimony of Jeffrey Lehman, Bench Trial, v. 5 p. 115 l.14 (Jan. 22, 2002) *Grutter v. Bollinger* (No. 02-241).

school admissions policy had much the same effect as the UC-Davis quota system in *Bakke*—excluding large numbers of white applicants to the benefit of preferred minorities. Over the two-year period of 1994–95, for example, among white applicants with LSAT scores between 154 and 169 and UGPAs between 3.25 and 4.0, 379 out of 1,437 were accepted. In the same ranges, 48 out of 52 blacks were accepted.[46] The plaintiff's expert witness, Dr. Kinley Larntz, a professor emeritus in the Department of Applied Statistics at the University of Minnesota, examined the admissions grid for the years 1995–2000, grouping applicants with similar LSAT and UGPA results into "cells" and then calculating the likelihood of acceptance based on race and ethnicity. He concluded that "membership in certain ethnic groups is an extremely strong factor in the decision for acceptance. Native American, African American, Mexican American, and Puerto Rican applicants in the same LSAT and GPA grid cell as a Caucasian American applicant have odds of acceptance that is many, many (tens to hundreds) times that of a similarly situated Caucasian American applicant."[47] This interpretation was challenged only at the margins by the law school and, to all intents and purposes, was later accepted as accurate by the U.S. Supreme Court.

Faculty discussions about the 1992 document are also revealing. An earlier draft, after embracing the benefits of diversity, included the following language: "Also it is important to note that in the past we seem to have achieved the kinds of benefits that we associate with racial and ethnic diversity from classes in which the proportion of African American, Hispanic and Native American members has been

---

46. *Grutter*, 137 F. Supp. 2d at 832.
47. *Id.* at 836.

between about 11% and 17% of enrollees." The language was excluded from the final draft as "too rigid," meaning it "could be misconstrued as a quota."[48]

Another faculty member proposed a 20 percent limit on "non-grid admittees" who were admitted for reasons of race, arguing that the "target range" should be spelled out "for a variety of reasons, including candor."[49] His proposal was also voted down.

These actions had the desired effect, providing school deans and lesser officials with the opportunity to defend "critical mass" without embracing quotas. On the stand, none could say what numbers constituted such a mass, though Dennis Shields, a former admissions dean, suggested that 5 percent might be too low.[50] Although daily tabulations were kept as to the number of minorities agreeing to enroll, all professed the numbers had no impact on any particular decisions. Nor did any acknowledge that the process of admission by race had the unintended effect of forcing students to regard themselves as identified primarily by race and ethnicity. This despite the formations of law student associations identified as black, Hispanic, Christian, Jewish, and even Arab.

There was one final virtue of diversity as a justification for race preferences that was well-captured by Judge Duggan in his opinion upholding the more rigid LSA program: "Furthermore, unlike the remedial setting, diversity in higher education, by its very nature, is a permanent and ongoing interest. . . . Therefore, unlike the remedial setting, where the need for remedial action terminates once the effects of past

48. *Id.* at 835.
49. *Id.*
50. *Id.* at 832.

discrimination have been eradicated, the need for diversity lives on perpetually."[51]

In fairness, the Michigan leadership, at least at the outset of the litigation, believed they were fighting to retain meaningful minority representation in their school. In his testimony, law school dean Jeffrey Lehman—who has since accepted the presidency of Cornell—mentioned UC-Berkeley's Boalt Hall, which he described as a great public institution once similar in many respects to Michigan, but no longer. "Since the adoption of the Regents' policy and ultimately Proposition 209, as a voter issue in California we had seen dramatic reduction in the number of under-represented minority students at Boalt Hall. And that has persisted over time. It's fallen to what I would describe as a token level."[52] This was true of the law schools at UCLA and Texas, too. "[T]hese are very smart people. They are doing everything they can and they have not gotten beyond token levels of African-Americans at either of those schools."[53] This was a steady theme expressed by Michigan and its advocates throughout the litigation: Minority representation at the school would crash like California and Texas if race preferences were tossed out. Clearly, Lehman was correct, assuming that the law school would meekly abandon its race preference system without seeking to circumvent it. In the year 2000, for example, although 35 percent of minority law school applicants were accepted, the school estimated that in the absence of affirmative action the number would have been 10 percent—a dramatic drop.[54]

51. *Grutter*, 137 F. Supp. 2d at 824.
52. Testimony of Jeffrey Lehman, Bench Trial v. 5 p. 142 l.22.
53. *Id.*
54. *Grutter*, 137 F. Supp. 2d at 839.

The principal argument against percentage plans was offered in the companion LSA case by William G. Bowen, co-author of *The Shape of the River*. According to Bowen, the school would favor unprepared students from poor high schools who manage to finish in the top 10 percent of their class "while turning down better-prepared applicants who happen not to finish in the top tenth of their class in academically stronger schools."[55] But wouldn't these students bring precisely—and far more honestly—the very diversity of outlook and experience that Bowen and Bok so cherished as the cargo of overprivileged African American students? It seems that no one had a keener appreciation for academic merit than Bowen and Bok, at least when the subject was anything other than race preferences.

The plaintiffs and Michigan were not the only parties to the case. A group of seventeen minority students who had applied or intended to apply to the university sought to intervene as defendants, claiming they were entitled to special admissions consideration to redress the effects of both present and past discrimination. Represented by the NAACP Legal Defense Fund and its brilliant attorney Ted Shaw and supported by such academic heavyweights as the distinguished historian John Hope Franklin and Harvard's education and race specialist Gary Orfield, the group hoped to demonstrate an entitlement to special treatment based on both the lingering effects of such institutions as slavery and segregation and the residual impact of racism and discrimination in such areas as housing, employment, standardized tests, and K–12 education. They were, of course, running into the teeth of recent judicial precedent, which tended to regard past discrimination as too amorphous to support relief. Pres-

---

55. *Gratz*, 122 F. Supp. 2d at 830.

ent discrimination is usually treated judicially as an act against individuals who can, in most cases, be rendered whole through damages and declaratory relief. The district court's ruling against intervention was reversed on appeal.[56] The intervenors never got close to a favorable ruling on the merits and were foreclosed from arguing their case before the Supreme Court because Michigan objected to splitting their time, and the justices agreed.

On March 27, 2001, U.S. District Court Judge Bernard A. Friedman found the law school plan unconstitutional. "The evidence shows that race is not as defendants have argued merely one factor which is considered among many others in the admissions process," he declared. "Rather the evidence indisputably demonstrates that the law school places a very heavy emphasis on an applicant's race in deciding whether to accept or reject."[57] Although critical mass had eluded precise quantification, in practice, it meant that 10–17 percent of each class would be preferred minority. Year in and year out, the preferred minorities were admitted in nearly the precise percentages as their numbers in the applicant pool. The dean and admissions director followed the progress of minority acceptances in the school's "daily admissions reports" to see how close to target the minorities were.

Judge Friedman set for himself the task of deciding whether *Bakke* stood for the proposition that diversity is a compelling interest opening the door for a narrowly tailored race-conscious admissions policy. Clearly that was Justice Powell's view, but no other justice had joined the part of his opinion in which he had articulated it. The so-called Brennan

56. *Grutter v. Bollinger*, 188 F.3d 394 (6th Cir. 1999).
57. *Grutter*, 137 F. Supp. 2d at 840.

group of Brennan, Blackmun, Marshall, and White, who joined Powell in striking down the California Supreme Court injunction against any consideration of race, never mentioned diversity in their opinion, insisting that benign discrimination calculated to address the effects of centuries of discrimination should not be subject to strict judicial scrutiny. Even so, Michigan argued that the case of *Marks v. United States* should control, because *Marks* held that where no single position commands the vote of five justices, the holding of the court should be that which rests on the narrowest of grounds. Unfortunately, wrote Judge Friedman, though the *Bakke* court had divided in three *different* ways, none was more broad or narrow than the other, and thus *Marks* could not come into play.[58] Thus, there was effectively no *Bakke* precedent, and the courts had to apply more recent Supreme Court pronouncements in such cases as *Croson* and *Adarand*. The race-conscious policies in those cases gained approval only to redress well-defined past discrimination. The court did not doubt that diversity bestows educational benefits that are both "important and laudable. Nonetheless, the fact remains that the attainment of a racially diverse class is not a compelling state interest because it was not recognized as such by *Bakke* and is not a remedy for past discrimination."[59]

Even had the school succeeded in establishing a compelling interest, the law school would have failed because "critical mass" was an amorphous concept with no time limit that effectively set aside places for preferred groups and offered no logical reason for including some and not including others. Why did the school think Puerto Ricans from New York

58. *Id.* at 844.
59. *Id.* at 850.

would contribute to diversity, while those from San Juan would not? Why were the views of Mexican Americans more pertinent than Nicaraguan Americans? Finally, the court found no exploration of race-neutral alternatives, such as "decreasing the emphasis for all applicants on undergraduate GPA and LSAT scores, using a lottery system for all qualified applicants, or a system whereby a certain percentage of the top graduates from various colleges and universities are admitted."[60]

Judge Friedman had had to put his foot down to keep the case. Early in the proceedings, the university had moved to consolidate the two cases before Judge Duggan, a Democratic appointee, thus taking the case from Judge Friedman, a Republican appointee. Chief Judge Anna Diggs Taylor recused herself from considering the motion because her husband sat on the school's board of trustees. Instead of stepping back entirely and allowing a random method of selecting the judge to rule on the motion, however, she appointed two like-thinking judges who promptly declared the two suits "companion cases" suitable for Judge Duggan, despite the fact that both involved totally different admissions systems. Under Michigan law, however, the final word belonged to Judge Friedman, who tartly rejected the idea. In the end, he ruled against the law school, while Judge Duggan held for LSA in the undergraduate case. Together they found the exact opposite of how matters would be decided by the U.S. Supreme Court. This was not the last bit of procedural trickery that courts sympathetic to Michigan would engage in, though one suspects that in a case of this magnitude the only court disposition that really would matter would be that of the Supreme Court of the United States.

60. *Id.* at 852–853.

Chapter Seven

The Sixth Circuit

Chief Judge Boyce F. Martin, Jr., could have joined the judicial debate over race preferences and college admissions with an opinion that probed both undergraduate and law school practices at the University of Michigan against the equal protection standard of the Fifth Amendment. He could have meticulously reviewed the evidence gathered or acknowledged, including recent Supreme Court pronouncements, the supporting study undertaken by Patricia Gurin, its critique elaborated by amici and opposing counsel. He might have staked out new ground, as the appellate court had done in *Hopwood*, or stuck doggedly to the law as had Judge Stanley Marcus in *Johnson*. Instead, Judge Martin did none of these things. He merely declared, at the urging of Michigan, that the court was bound by the decision in the interstate pornography case *Marks v. United States*.[1] *Marks* had, in turn, interpreted the Court's holding in a case involving the famous bawdy tale by John Cleland, *Memoirs of a*

---

1. *Marks v. United States*, 430 U.S. 188 (1977).

Woman of Pleasure, in the case of *Memoirs v. Massachusetts*.[2]
The question in *Marks* was which Supreme Court pronounce-
ment controlled the definition of obscenity when no previous
definition had commanded a five-vote majority. In *Memoirs*,
three justices, led by the irrepressible William Brennan, held
that for a work to be obscene it must be "utterly without
redeeming social value."[3] Justice Potter Stewart declared the
novel not obscene because it was not hard-core pornography,
while Justices Black and Douglas—absolutists on the First
Amendment—held that any restriction on the printed word
violated its terms.[4] In *Marks*, the Court embraced the Brennan
standard, holding that "[w]hen a fragmented Court decides a
case and no single rationale explaining the result enjoys the
assent of five Justices, the holding of the Court may be viewed
as that position taken by those Members who concurred in
the judgment on the narrowest of grounds."[5] To Judge Martin
and the four Sixth Circuit jurists who agreed with him, this
meant that Justice Powell's *Bakke* views were still the law of
the land and that diversity was a compelling state need that
could be reflected in race-conscious admissions practices.
The slender majority then proceeded to accept every material
Michigan statement, from the lack of efficacy of race-neutral
policies to the absence of any fixed number or percentage of
minorities considered each year. The court thus reversed the
decision of District Court Judge Friedman and declared the
law school practice legally identical to the Harvard Plan out-
lined by Powell. The Sixth Circuit would also later hold the
undergraduate admissions program legal, but not until the

---

2. *Memoirs of a Woman of Pleasure v. Massachusetts*, 383 U.S. 413 (1966).
3. *Id*. at 427.
4. *Id*. at 433.
5. *Marks*, 430 U.S. at 193.

Supreme Court had already taken jurisdiction and the parties had briefed and argued their case.

Had this been all, the Sixth Circuit ruling would hardly be worth a mention. However, a passionate concurrence by Judge Eric Lee Clay, an erudite dissent by Judge Danny Boggs, and a testy exchange initiated by Boggs over what he charged was Martin's irregular procedural handling of the case designed to keep control in Martin's own hands with the result to be determined by those sympathetic to affirmative action, all combined to make the proceedings of some interest.

Judge Clay stated:

> [It is] insulting to African Americans, or to any race or ethnicity that has known oppression and discrimination the likes of which slavery embodies, to think that a generation enjoying the end product of a life of affluence has forgotten or cannot relate the enormous personal sacrifice made by their family members and ancestors not all that long ago in order to make the end possible. We are only a generation removed from legally enforced segregation and the many denials embraced by the practice. Further, it is naïve to think that simply because a black person earns good money, resides in a fashionable apartment and shops at stores that cater to the rich, his or her life has been devoid of brushes with insult and discrimination that establish a common experiential bond among people of color. A well-dressed black woman of wealthy means shopping at Neiman Marcus or in an affluent shopping center may well be treated with the same suspect eye and bigotry as the poorly dressed black woman of limited means shopping at Target.[6]

The clear thrust of Clay's argument—even if he didn't say so in so many words—is that race is a proxy for experience

---

6. *Grutter*, 288 F.3d at 732, 764.

and that a university like Michigan is correct to award preferences to minority students. Judge Boggs's grudging offer in dissent to stipulate that race *does* matter "constitutes a thinly veiled offer of dubious sincerity, to say the least,"[7] particularly for those who have read the rest of Boggs's decision.

Clay then emulated what had become a favorite tactic of race preference apologists, going back at least to *The Shape of the River*—pushing the notion that whites are not hurt by the preferences granted to minorities. Bowen and Bok had suggested that eliminating affirmative action at the twenty-eight selective schools they examined would have increased the percentage of white undergraduate applicant acceptances from 25 percent to 26.5 percent. Judge Clay offered this bit of shocking information: "The Mellon Foundation, which sponsored the study, provided me with additional data to calculate the admission rates by SAT score. If the schools in the Bowen/Bok sample had admitted applicants with similar SAT scores at the same rate regardless of race, the chance of admission for white applicants would have increased by one percentage point or less at scores of 1300 and above, by three to four percentage points at scores from 1150 to 1299, and by four to seven percentage points at scores below 1150."[8]

This was shocking to begin with because it is both odd and unethical for Judge Clay to have scampered outside the voluminous record of the case for his own private evidentiary service, compliments of the Mellon Foundation. Suppose that in the appeal from a murder conviction Judge Clay had written, "The prosecution claim of supporting DNA evidence is phony. At my request, the XYZ Laboratory ran its own analysis of the defendant's DNA and compared it to the evi-

7. *Id.* at 765.
8. *Id.* at 767.

dence acquired at the crime scene. XYZ found no match."
Pretty shabby behavior, most would agree, and no less shabby
in the Michigan case.

Nor are the Mellon/Clay figures particularly persuasive.
For one thing, the Constitution does not deal in group rights
but in individual rights. It is no more acceptable to trample
the rights of a single person than it is a larger group. One
suspects that if Judge Clay were to discover that the Detroit
police were giving backroom beatings to 1 percent of black
suspects accused of stealing $1,100, 3 to 4 percent accused
of stealing $1,200, and 4 to 7 percent accused of stealing more
than $1,300, he'd be pretty upset. Conveniently, too, the Bok/
Mellon/Clay figures ignore the existence of Asian Americans
who, no less than whites, are victims of Michigan's academic
race preferences and who are no less entitled to Constitutional protection. Also, the figures are far more substantial
than Judge Clay would have us believe. In the four years from
1995 to 1998, the law school admitted 183 underrepresented
minorities. Assuming, as Michigan had estimated, that three
out of four of these would not have gotten in on their academic merits, some 138 whites and Asian Americans were
kept out over that four-year period for reasons of race. This
does not even address what was going on in the undergraduate program, which handles five times the volume of law
school applications. Nor does it take into account the tens of
thousands of youngsters who apply to other selective colleges
and universities every year. In short, the notion that African
American and Hispanic students can be assisted while
whites are virtually unharmed and Asian Americans functionally cease to exist is insulting. This was perhaps shown
most vividly in oral argument when, in response to questions
from Judge Boggs, Michigan's counsel acknowledged that
had Barbara Grutter been black, she would likely have won

admission to the law school. He hastened to add, however, that a Barbara Grutter who was black "would be a different person."[9]

"This case involves a straightforward instance of racial discrimination by a state institution," began Judge Boggs in his memorable dissent.[10] He rejected the mass of circumlocutions designed to obscure this fact, recalling Orwell's complaint in *Politics and the English Language* that too often "a mass of Latin words falls upon the facts like snow, blurring the outline and covering up all the details."[11] In Grutter, the problem was not Latin words but the attempt by the law school to escape the consequences of *Bakke* by changing form, not substance. Yet the content of the policy was clear. From 1995 to 1998, the law school admitted between forty-four and forty-seven preferred minority students, 13.5 to 13.7 percent of each entering class. "For me, however, the Law School's simple avoidance of an explicit numerical target does not meet the constitutional requirements of narrow tailoring. The Law School's efforts to achieve a 'critical mass' are functionally indistinguishable from a numerical quota."[12] Moreover, the diversity rationale is spurious. In its literature, the university exalts various types of diversity, but in practice, only the narrowest kind of racial and ethnic distinctions amounts to very much. "The Law School's rhetoric implies that it is searching tirelessly for the applicant with the most unique of experiences: for example, the Mormon missionary in Uganda, the radical libertarian or Marxist, the child of subsistence farmers in Arkansas, or perhaps the professional

---

9. *Id.* at 775.
10. *Id.* at 773.
11. *Id.*
12. *Id.* at 789.

jazz musician. The Law School, however, never claims that there is any similarity between the preference given to those with such unique experiences and that bestowed upon those it considers 'under-represented' racial minorities.'"[13] In the school's literature, the unrelenting search for diversity may reward the applicant with "an Olympic gold medal, a Ph.D. in physics, the attainment of age 50 in a class otherwise lacking anyone over 30, or the experience of having been a Vietnamese boat person."[14] Such lyricism, however, usually remains on the pages of the law school's *Admissions Policies* booklet, while the admissions dean and her advisors zero in on race and ethnicity. "The figures indicate that race is worth over one full grade point of college average or at least an 11-point and 20 percentile boost on the LSAT. In effect, the Law School admits students by giving very substantial additional weight to virtually every candidate designated as an 'under-represented minority', or equivalently, by substantially discounting the credentials earned by every student who happens to fall outside the Law School's minority designation. . . . The Law School's admission practices betray its claim that it gives meaningful individual consideration to every applicant, notwithstanding their race."[15]

Judge Boggs saw a dangerous parallel between Michigan's emulation of the Harvard Plan and a Harvard Plan that had been imposed in the 1930s to limit the number of Jews attending the university so as to more accurately reflect their percentage of the population. "The reasons for the policy offered by then-President Lowell of Harvard are hauntingly similar to the rationale given here. As Lowell explained, without the

13. *Id.* at 790.
14. *Id.*
15. *Id.* at 797–798.

policies, 'Harvard would lose its character as a democratic national university drawing from all classes of the community and promoting sympathetic understanding among them.'"[16] If the grave disparities between the percentage of Jews in the population at large and their percentage of the Harvard student body could be addressed, "it would eliminate race feeling among the students, and as these students passed out into the world, eliminating it in the community."[17]

Judge Boggs also considered the public claim by veteran civil rights activist Julian Bond that racial preferences for blacks are the "just spoils of a righteous war," the long battle for African American rights in America.[18] Not so, said Boggs. If, as Lincoln wrote in his Second Inaugural Address, "society chooses that 'every drop of blood drawn by the lash shall be paid by another,' then that bill should be paid by the whole society, and by the considered alteration of our Equal Protection Clause, not by ignoring it."[19] He also recalled the pre-*Brown* plaintiff, Heman Sweatt, whom the Court ordered admitted to the University of Texas Law School after the school had first rejected him entirely and then sought to instruct him in a law school cobbled together for the sole purposes of diverting blacks from the flagship state university. "Michigan's plan does not seek diversity for education's sake. It seeks racial numbers for the sake of the comfort that those abstract numbers may bring. It does so at the expense of the real rights of real people to fair consideration. It is a long road from Heman Sweatt to Barbara Grutter. But they

16. *Id.* at 793–794.
17. *Id.*
18. *Id.* at 809.
19. *Id.*

both ended up outside a door that a government's use of racial considerations denied them a fair chance to enter."[20]

Judge Boggs added a Procedural Appendix to his dissent, accusing Chief Judge Martin, a Democrat appointee, with improperly manipulating the docket, the suggestion being that Martin sought to ensure a majority would vote to uphold Michigan's admission policies.[21] In April 2001, as the case first reached the appellate court, Judge Martin had assigned it to a three-judge panel—including himself—rather than using the more traditional random assignment methods. According to Judge Boggs, the Chief Judge also knew, but didn't inform his colleagues, that Michigan had moved to have the case heard by the entire circuit court sitting en banc. At the time, the court boasted eleven members, but Judges Norris and Suhrheinrich, both appointed by Republican presidents, were scheduled to achieve "senior status," which meant retirement from most functions, including participation in en banc arguments. In October 2001, days before the case was scheduled for argument before the three-judge panel, and long after opening briefs had been filed, the remaining six judges were informed the case would be heard en banc before a panel where six of the judges had been appointed by Democrats.

Judge Karen Nelson Moore, who voted with the majority on the merits of the case, rebuked Boggs for what she called his "inaccurate and misleading account of the procedural facts underlying the present case."[22] Her basic point was that the timing of the two judges' retirements was such that they would have been off the bench even had notice of the en banc

20. *Id.* at 810.
21. *Id.* at 811.
22. *Id.* at 753.

petition been more promptly circulated. By that time, however, tempers were frayed. Judge Clay, for example, concurring with the majority opinion, said he found it necessary to
write separately "for the purpose of speaking to the misrep-
resentations made by Judge Boggs in his dissenting opinion
which unjustifiably distort and seek to cast doubt on the
majority opinion."[23]

The allegation of misconduct soon became the subject of
a complaint filed by the activist group Judicial Watch and its
president, Thomas Fitton.[24] In May 2003, Acting Chief Judge
Alice M. Batchelder ruled that Judge Martin had failed to
follow his own established rules both in assigning the three-
judge case to himself and, later, by failing to inform colleagues of the en banc petition in a timely fashion. According
to Judge Batchelder, Martin's actions "raise an inference that
wrongdoing has occurred."[25] Without minimizing the seri-
ousness of Martin's judicial tricks, it is reasonable to assume
that however the Sixth Circuit had ruled, the case would
speedily have made its way to the Supreme Court given the
importance of the subject and the split among several judicial
circuits.

For his part, Judge Boggs's opinion was written with the
self-confidence of one drawn by the wake of prevailing
Supreme Court precedent, particularly as articulated by
Justice Sandra Day O'Connor. Boggs cited Justice O'Connor
in *Croson*: "Classifications based on race carry a danger of
stigmatic harm. Unless they are strictly reserved for remedial
settings, they may in fact promote notions of racial inferiority

23. *Id.* at 758.

24. Letter from Thomas Fitton, president of Judicial Watch, to circuit executive
of the Sixth Circuit (Jan. 30, 2003). *See* Jodi S. Cohen, *Judicial Bias Alleged in
U-M Case*, DETROIT NEWS, Mar. 30, 2003.

25. Cohen, *Judicial Misconduct*, at 1A.

and lead to a politics of racial hostility."[26] Further, remedial race-conscious measures must have a "logical stopping point."[27] Finally, O'Connor had voted to overturn *Metro Broadcasting* with its diversity rationale.

It was not Judge Boggs, but rather the Center for New Black Leadership that, in its amicus brief, reminded the court of Justice O'Connor's most pointed condemnation of equating race with viewpoint. In the redistricting case *Shaw v. Reno*, she wrote that such thinking bears "an uncomfortable resemblance to apartheid. It reinforces the perception that members of the same racial group—regardless of their age, education, economic status, or the community in which they live—think alike, share the same political interests, and will prefer the same candidates at the polls. We have rejected such perceptions elsewhere as impermissible racial stereotypes."[28]

Cavalier court management and the resultant majority of judicial liberals may have put Judge Boggs in the minority on Michigan on the Sixth Circuit, but there was every reason to believe he would be vindicated on appeal with Justice O'Connor writing the majority opinion.

26. *Grutter*, 288 F.3d at 787.
27. *Id.* at 793.
28. *Shaw v. Reno*, 590 U.S. 630, 647 (1993).

Chapter Eight

Argument

Supreme Court argument on the two Michigan cases was held on April Fools' Day, after a cold blustery night that left many who had camped where they stood in line in the hope of getting a cherished seat in the courtroom shaking as much from the chill as from anticipation. Demonstrators, most of them supporters of race preferences, urged the Court to save affirmative action. Some attacked the justices themselves for failing to hire black law clerks, perhaps signaling a note of irony that this venerable institution—as merit conscious as any in the nation—was being asked by the university to allow academic merit to take a back seat to race.

The cases would be argued separately but successively, with *Grutter*, the law school case, at 10:00 A.M., and *Gratz*, involving undergraduate admissions, at 11:00. Kolbo's burden of arguing both cases while Mahoney and Payton divided the task of defending Michigan was eased somewhat by the presence of Solicitor General Theodore B. Olson, who sought to persuade the Court that both the law school and the undergraduate admissions practices were unconstitutional. A brilliant advocate, Olson was still basking in the glow of his victory in *Bush v. Gore*, the case that decided the presidency. As a private practitioner, Olson had argued and won the *Hopwood* case, where he had convinced the Fifth Circuit Court of Appeals to declare *Bakke* a dead letter and race-conscious admissions illegal. He had urged the Bush administration to take a similar position in these cases, but the White House had demurred, instructing him to argue simply that both the law school and undergraduate admissions policies were functional quotas that violated the *Bakke* standard. Thus, Olson argued in brief that "this case requires this Court to break no new ground"[1] and to merely hold Michigan's practices unconstitutional as disguised quotas that were not narrowly tailored since the same diversity could be achieved with race-neutral alternatives. Indeed, the Olson brief went so far as to list a smorgasbord of admissions criteria that a school could apply to candidates to promote racial and ethnic diversity, including "a history of overcoming disadvantage, geographic origin, socioeconomic status, challenging living or family situations, reputation and location of high schools, volunteer work experiences, exceptional personal talents, leadership potential, communication skills, commitment and dedication to particular causes, extracurricular activities, extraordinary expertise in a particular area, and individual outlook as reflected in essays."[2] In other words, the more opaque the process, the greater the likelihood of winding up with the desired racial and ethnic mix without ever purporting to consider race or ethnicity. Texas, California, and Florida were held out not only as models but also as road maps

---

1. Brief for the United States as Amicus Curiae Supporting Petitioner at 10, *Grutter v. Bollinger*, 123 S. Ct. 2325 (2003) (No. 02-241).
     2. *Id.* at 19.

to follow lest one crash through the barricades of unconstitutional race consciousness.

Kolbo approached his argument like a fighter with a very logical but inflexible battle plan whose strength could be dissipated by an unorthodox or unanticipated counterattack. He began by stating that Barbara Grutter had been denied her constitutional rights when race was employed to tip the scales against her. Justice O'Connor was waiting. "Is your position that [race] cannot be one of many factors?"[3] Kolbo responded in the affirmative.

Justice O'Connor already seemed intent upon clearing the obstacles from a path she might choose to follow. The Court has allowed the consideration of race in "certain contexts," she reminded him, for example, as a remedy for past discrimination.

Kolbo acknowledged that was the case. Then this was not a question of absolutes, said Justice O'Connor. "I think we have given recognition to the use of race in a variety of settings."[4]

Was this the same justice who had been so categorical in limiting the applicability of race in cases like *Croson, Metro Broadcasting,* and *Shaw?* As opponents of race preferences had feared, Justice O'Connor's support could no longer be taken for granted.

Justice Kennedy entered the conversation with one of the ultimate considerations of the case—the paucity of minority candidates qualified to compete as equals for places at the law school. "Suppose you have a law school with two or three

---

3. Transcript of Oral Argument at 3, *Grutter v. Bollinger,* 123 S. Ct. 2325 (2003) (No. 02-241).

4. *Id.* at 4.

percent Hispanic and black students, is that a legitimate concern for the university and for the state officials?"[5]

Kolbo said there was no "right number for each racial
group," and he was probably right. However, a critical early
chance to make a key point escaped him, never to surface in
the oral argument and to appear only in Justice Scalia's later
dissent. No, the state of Michigan has no interest, let alone a
compelling one, in the number of minorities at the elite
national law school because the university places little if any
priority on feeding its distinguished graduates into practice
there. Only about a quarter of each class comes from Michigan; fewer than that go on to practice in the state—in contrast,
say, to Detroit's Wayne State University, which sends three-
quarters of its graduates into Michigan practice. The only
compelling interest issue was Justice Powell's acceptance of
the limited right of each school to define the contribution of
racial and ethnic diversity to the educational environment.

Kolbo would have to contend with another brief, one to
which he had paid scant attention in preparing for his oral
argument. Put together with the active behind-the-scenes
intervention of Secretary of State Colin Powell, a group of
twenty-eight retired military officers, national security officials, and present and former members of the United States
Senate, the so-called "Green Brief" urged that military necessity required substantial representation from African American and other minorities in the officer corps.[6] The brief
contended that, with the military more than 20 percent African American, it cannot afford another Vietnam period where
fewer than 3 percent of the officers were black. Morale dete-

---

5. *Id.*
6. Consolidated Brief of Lt. Gen. Julius W. Becton et al., as Amici Curiae in
Support of Respondents, *Grutter v. Bollinger*, 123 S. Ct. 2325 (2003) (No. 02-241).

riorated. The military was "on the verge of self-destruction," so it decided to change. It has changed. However, in the military, as in so many other settings, the strict application of merit to the award of ROTC scholarships and admission to the service academies would result in the functional exclusion of blacks. "At present no alternative exists to limited, race-conscious programs to increase the pool of high quality minority officer candidates and to establish diverse educational settings for officers."[7]

Justice Ginsburg introduced the "Green Brief" to the argument, an instrument with which Kolbo would be pilloried for many valuable noncontiguous minutes, reminding the counsel that its authors saw no way of satisfying their defense needs without affirmative action. Kolbo pleaded for mercy. The issue of the brief was not one between the parties to the case; there was no record developed below to warrant discussion. Yet Justice Ginsburg was relentless and Kolbo tepidly offered that "other solutions could be looked at addressing the problem why there are not minorities in the military."[8] Neither the United States nor the military academies had taken a position on the issue in this case.

However, according to Justices Stevens and Souter, the military academies did practice race consciousness. Again Kolbo pleaded no record below. Justice Scalia tried to rescue Kolbo, suggesting that race-neutral remedies, like socioeconomic condition, could help the academies, but Souter held on like a bulldog. Suppose the military did come up with other factors. Souter asked, "Do you seriously believe that that would be anything but a surrogate to race? It would take race out of the categorization of the label that we put on it,

7. *Id.* at 7.
8. *Id.* at 6.

but do you believe it would function in a different way but as a surreptitious approach to race?"[9]

From the day of their first moot court or appellate practice argument in law school, attorneys are trained never to dismiss a question from the bench as irrelevant, no matter how irrelevant it is. The judges collectively will take offense. They will settle scores with you and, through you, your client. Yet some questions are wide of the mark, as was the entire colloquy on the military brief. Not only was no record made below, as Kolbo noted, but also, he might have gone on to say, a situation involving the national security of the United States stands on a different footing from the case at bar. In the name of national security, this society has abided the suspension of habeas corpus proceedings, major encroachments on free speech and association, the forced relocation of American citizens of Japanese descent, and very recently the denial of the right of an Air Force officer who happened to be an Orthodox Jew to wear a yarmulke on the job.[10] So whatever decision is made in the Michigan case should not apply to the service academies or to the ROTC programs. Let the president, as commander-in-chief, determine the level of race consciousness needed to sustain these institutions in optimum fashion. At such time as the president's determination is challenged, the Court can look at the matter and decide it on its own, quite apart from any decision in the instant case.

Instead, Kolbo found himself engaged with Justice Kennedy on the constitutionality of race consciousness in the recruitment of minority academy candidates or for training programs designed to prepare them to score well on the

9. *Id.* at 9.
10. *Booker v. Gilless*, 67 Fed. Appx. 860 (6th Cir. 2003).

entrance exams. Kolbo said he had no problem with that. "Casting a wider net" was fine as long as race consciousness was dropped "at the point of competition" among candidates.[11] Kolbo would walk all over himself with that point, but later conceded that a racially exclusive scholarship was okay, "[b]ecause it doesn't prevent someone from applying. The key is to be able to compete on the same footing at the point of competition."[12] Justice Scalia finally rescued Kolbo, drawing agreement that a segregated preparatory program would be constitutionally troublesome. By that point, however, Kolbo probably felt as though he had been through an unforeseen crash course in military personnel practices.

On occasion, Kolbo would score a point. For example, when Justice Breyer wandered through a long dissertation on the need for efforts to rescue minority children from de facto segregated inferior schools and wondered why race cannot be a factor in educating the students, military officers, and businesspeople who would one day break the spell, Kolbo was direct and eloquent in reply: "Because, very simply, Justice Breyer, the Constitution provides . . . individuals with the right of equal protection. And by discriminating on the basis of race at a point of competition, innocent individuals are being injured in their constitutional rights."[13] But just as suddenly Kolbo ended up back in the midst of the military muddle. When presented with a hypothetical question that he might have anticipated, he took such a hard line as to seem inflexible. Justice Ginsburg confronted him with just such a question about a hypothetical prison with a large minority population "and the state wanted to give a preference so that

11. Transcript of Oral Argument at 9, *Grutter.*
12. *Id.* at 13.
13. *Id.* at 12.

it would have a critical mass of correction officers of the minority race, that would be impermissible?"[14]

Kolbo's reply: "It would be impermissible, Your Honor, unless based upon a compelling interest and the only one that has been recognized in the employment context is identified discrimination. And I don't see that in your hypothetical."[15]

A better response: The key here is to recruit and hire a diverse police or prison guard force using race-neutral methods that have worked throughout the country. Included would be Spanish-speaking officers or others who had grown up or lived in heavily minority areas—both of which are legitimate qualifications for officers dealing with concentrated minority populations. In fact, geographic affirmative action would be critical here since the prisons are often located in rural white areas, while most of the inmates come from the inner cities. The mistake would be to atone for poor planning by parachuting in at the eleventh hour to beg that a compelling need exists for discriminatory hiring.

But Kolbo wasn't up to it.

Olson tried to save an argument that was badly off course. "The Michigan Law School admissions program fails every test this Court has articulated for evaluating government racial preferences," he began.[16] But he too became sidetracked on the Green Brief issues as the clock ticked on.

Then, after an exchange with Justice Breyer over whether the law school's approach reinforced or dispelled racial stereotypes, Justice O'Connor weighed in with the last question that Olson wanted to hear. "General Olson, do you—do you

14. *Id.* at 16.
15. *Id.*
16. *Id.* at 17.

agree with the articulated proposal of Justice Powell in the *Bakke* case of using race as a plus-factor as he—as he saw the use of it? Do you disagree with that approach?"[17]

Olson couldn't answer the question substantively without taking a position on the issue President Bush had instructed him to avoid, the correctness of *Bakke*. Olson tried to dodge by raising the issue of whether Justice Powell's lonely opinion had really enjoyed the imprimatur of the Court, but Justice O'Connor wouldn't let him get away with that and asked him again whether he agreed with Powell's approach.

Olson waffled again, returning to the claim that even Justice Powell's standard had been exceeded by Michigan, but the liberals on the Court persisted. Justice Stevens asked him whether he agreed with Justice Powell's use of the Harvard Plan as a model for race consciousness. Olson started to dismiss the suggestion that the Harvard Plan was examined under a compelling interest lens, but caught himself, perhaps remembering that Justice Powell had attached the plan to his opinion that diversity could be a compelling interest, or at least one that schools could pursue under their First Amendment rights.

After a brief discussion with Justice Breyer over the Texas "top ten" plan, in which the justice suggested that the plan differed only in disguise from what Olson was protesting in Michigan, Olson was finished. Having been hog-tied by the White House to the point where he could not maintain an intelligent conversation about *Bakke*, he had not done much to retrieve the situation he had inherited from Kolbo, who would love to have seen *Bakke* reversed but who had to downplay that to stay on the same page as his colleague.

17. *Id.* at 22.

Now it was Mahoney's turn. Mahoney knew that if five justices decided to overturn *Bakke*, she was dead. Sensing that was unlikely, however, she simply assumed, for purposes of her argument, that Powell's *Bakke* views were still good law and argued that the law school's admission practice was more like the Powell plus factor than the sixteen-place quota for minority medical students the *Bakke* court had rejected. This was not a program of fixed numbers or even ranges, she maintained. "[W]hat has occurred over the years with this program is that there have been offers that have ranged from 160 to 232 over the course of eight years, there have been enrollments that went from 44 to 73. It has been a very flexible program."[18]

Justice Scalia, the point man for anti–race preference sentiment on the Court, then launched an argument of his own that made technical sense but that presented the entire issue in a way that would be anathema to educators from coast to coast. Justice Scalia said he found it hard to take seriously the state's claim that its diversity need was sufficiently compelling "to warrant ignoring the Constitution's prohibition of distribution on the basis of race." After all, the problem had been generated by Michigan itself by deciding "to create an elite law school." That meant taking students from an academic level where few minorities are to be found. "Now if Michigan really cares enough about that racial imbalance, why doesn't it do as many other state law schools do, lower the standards, not have a flagship elite law school? It solves the problem."[19]

"Your Honor," Mahoney replied, "I don't think there's anything in this Court's cases that suggests that the law school

18. *Id.* at 28.
19. *Id.* at 29.

has to make an election between academic excellence and racial diversity."[20]

Justice Kennedy came to Justice Scalia's defense: "Where's the compelling interest? Isn't Michigan simply making a choice to provide a law school in a particular way and it doesn't have to do that?"

"But your Honor," Mahoney insisted, "there is a compelling interest in having an institution that is both academically excellent and racially diverse, because our leaders need to be trained in institutions that are excellent, that are superior academically, but they also need to be trained with exposure to the viewpoints, to the perspectives, to the experiences of individuals from diverse backgrounds."[21]

Technically, both Justices Scalia and Kennedy were right. Only a small handful of states—Michigan, California, Virginia—maintain top-rung public law schools, with North Carolina and Texas a notch below. Several states, New York included, maintain no public law schools at all. So Michigan's need in that narrow respect was hardly compelling. However, the problem is that the same argument can be made with respect to all elite schools, graduate and undergraduate, public and private, that maintain race-conscious programs. Harvard can become Hofstra and take in a class that is 10 percent African American with no affirmative action employed. Amherst can become Temple; Berkeley, Boise State. Fine and honorable schools, of course, but not the sort of metamorphosis to warm the heart of student or educator alike. Months later, even before the opinions came down, Michigan lawyers would chuckle when Justice Scalia's line of questioning was recalled, suggesting there wasn't a single

20. *Id.*
21. *Id.* at 30.

college president's office in the country where dumbing down to achieve race-neutral diversity would earn much of a hearing.

Next came one of those moments—precious to Supreme Court junkies—where both a justice and the counsel got their facts wrong on a very prominent case. Mahoney was in the midst of trying to convince Justice Kennedy that Michigan's numerical targets were more "aspirational" rather than quota-like in character, when Justice Ginsburg intervened to compare them with the Harvard Plan endorsed by Justice Powell in *Bakke*.

"Excuse me," interjected Justice Scalia. "Did *Bakke* hold that the Harvard plan was constitutional?"

Mahoney: "Yes, Your Honor."

Justice Scalia: "If adopted by—by a state institution?"

Mahoney: "Yes, Your Honor."

Justice Scalia: "It was held that it was constitutional?"

Mahoney: "Yes. What we . . ."

Justice Scalia: "We didn't even—We didn't even have the details of the Harvard Plan before us."

Mahoney: "Your Honor, in fact, the Court upheld—or Justice Powell appended the Harvard plan to his opinion in this case and there were fives votes that the reason that the mandate of the California supreme Court [enjoining the consideration of race in admissions] should be reversed was because there was an effective alternative for—for enrolling minorities and that effective alternative was a plan like the Harvard plan."[22]

Justice Scalia's mistake was evident and Mahoney promptly corrected him—the Harvard Plan was central to the Powell opinion and more than adequately described in and

22. *Id.* at 31–34.

appended to that opinion. But Mahoney's mistake was fundamental to an understanding of *Bakke* in two respects. First, Justice Powell never endorsed the Harvard Plan as an "effective alternative" to the quotas he rejected, but rather as a constitutional means of employing limited race consciousness to produce a diversity of viewpoint and experience in the class. Even more fundamental, the four justices who joined him in lifting the injunction against race-conscious admissions did so not on the basis of diversity but because, like private employers hiring blacks to cure the effects of historically segregated job categories, states may also adopt race-conscious programs designed to overcome substantial, chronic minority underrepresentation where there is reason to believe that the evil addressed is a product of past racial discrimination. Powell's rationale was rejected by his four brethren unless employed to redress past societal discrimination.

Just when Mahoney appeared to have tripped over her precedent, Justice Scalia returned with another bit of odd history, suggesting that "when the Harvard plan was originally adopted, its purpose was to achieve diversity by reducing the number of unusual students from New York that were getting into Harvard on the basis of merit alone."[23]

In fact, a number of prestigious institutions, including Harvard, contrived ways to hold down the number of New York Jews entering by virtue of academic merit, but that had occurred a generation before this Harvard Plan was born.

Justice Scalia finally found some solid footing by taking apart the claim that a "critical mass" with a range of 8 to 12 percent is any different from a 10 percent quota. However,

23. *Id.* at 33.

that was an issue so fundamental to the case that it is doubtful any opinions were going to be swayed by argument.

Of all the attributes of diversity for supporters of race-conscious admissions, the most marvelous is its lack of any inherent time constraint. When an employer hires blacks against whom he has previously discriminated, the ameliorative process stops when the victims of his discrimination are compensated and restored to their rightful employee status. When another hires blacks or Hispanics over whites to achieve a more balanced workforce in traditionally segregated job categories, that process too ends when the force comes to resemble the outside workforce in the relevant field. In each case, the discrimination involved is viewed as a necessary evil, finite in time, limited in impact on the majority race.

But this is not so with diversity, the theory of which is that diversity is a positive educational value benefiting students of all races and all ethnicities. It needs no past discrimination as justification. Michigan never discriminated; it admitted all students with the requisite academic credentials. In a race-blind system, Mahoney acknowledged, no blacks were admitted to the law school in 1964. In 2003, with race-blind admission procedures, only four would get in. Numbers like that provide their own justification for preferences in perpetuity. Michigan is not atoning, not ameliorating, not compensating—it is just educating.

However, Justice O'Connor seemed troubled by the timeless quality of the program. "Other affirmative action programs, you could see an end to it," she declared. "How do you deal with that aspect?"[24]

It could end, suggested Mahoney, either when there are

24. *Id.* at 39.

enough qualified minorities to drop the effort or when society evolves to the point "where the experience of being a minority did not make such a fundamental difference in their lives, where race didn't matter so much that it's truly salient to the law school's educational mission."[25] Yet she said nothing to suggest the imminence of either moment.

Mahoney argued that at Michigan, in general, only about 80 out of 2,500 admissions decisions were influenced by race, so, at worst, only 5 percent of white applicants were disadvantaged.

"I don't know any other area," Justice Scalia replied tartly, "where we decide the case by saying, well, there are very few people who are being treated unconstitutionally."[26]

The argument in *Gratz* was clearer cut because the issue was clearer cut. Michigan's undergraduate admissions program—with its separate admissions guidelines by race and ethnicity, protected or reserved seats, and segregated waiting lists—had initially resembled that of the University of Texas School of Law tossed out in *Hopwood*. During the trial below, Michigan had altered its method, now awarding a flat twenty-point bonus for preferred minority status, strikingly similar to the University of Georgia system rejected by the Court of Appeals for the Fourth Circuit. At trial, university officials had acknowledged that the purpose was to change the technique rather than the outcome of the process. In attacking a system on which he was nearly certain to prevail, however, Kolbo was able to reinforce his broader argument in both cases.

"The fundamental problem with the diversity rationale is that it depends on the standardless discretion of educa-

25. *Id.*
26. *Id.* at 52.

tors," he urged.[27] With any license to make race-conscious decisions for diversity's sake, the universities would be able to define the races and ethnic groups that they thought contributed most to the process. Out the window would go the critical process of strict scrutiny, which is essential in equal protection cases.

Both Kolbo and Olson could have done more with this concept to expose the practice for its corrupt infrastructure. At the time, Michigan was seeking to favor blacks, Hispanics, and Native Americans at the expense of whites and Asian Americans. The school claimed that this was a First Amendment academic right. Suppose, instead, that a state university determined that Jews were a particularly varied group in their intellectual development and political advocacy. Could the school admit Jews in numbers well beyond their academic credentials to the detriment of others? Or suppose a faculty committee determined that black social and political advocacy was as repetitive as a stuck needle and that black social and residential habits were limiting rather than enhancing student campus interaction. Could the university then ban blacks or lower their acceptance rates for purposes of academic diversity? Doesn't any race preference system become a de facto racial entitlement, even after it has supposedly gone away? Isn't that what "critical mass" is really all about? In fact, isn't the real lesson from Texas, California, and Florida that the notion of entitlement becomes so deeply fixed that it can even survive a change in the law? Drop the black numbers at Michigan five or ten years from now, and every civil rights advocate, every *New York Times*–reading liberal, would be crying foul.

27. Transcript of Oral Argument at 8, *Gratz v. Bollinger*, 123 S. Ct. 2411 (2003) (No. 02-516).

Given time to develop his argument without the distraction of the military brief, Olson made some cogent points. For instance, he articulated the contradiction inherent in the diversity rationale whose supporters claim that first we must admit you because your experience living in this society provides you with a common focus on events, but we must also admit enough of you so our white students will see how different you are from one another.

Olson was also at his most effective in responding to Justice Ginsburg, who noted a desirable race consciousness in places like Canada, the European Union, and South Africa. Olson's reply: "I submit, Justice Ginsburg, that none of those countries has our history, none of those countries has the Fourteenth Amendment, none of those countries has the history of statements by this Court which has examined the question over and over again that the ultimate damage that is done by racial preferences is such that if there ever is a situation which such factors must be used that they must be—race neutral means must be tried to accomplish those objectives, narrow tailoring must be applied, and this—this—these fail all of those tests."[28]

Justice Kennedy provided the coda for the *Gratz* argument, declaring, "I have to say that in—in looking at your program it looks to me like this is just a disguised quota."[29]

Both sets of attorneys came out of the oral argument with a sense of optimism. Kolbo and his colleagues felt the undergraduate Michigan scheme was dead and buried and that the law school's "critical mass" was so quota-like in character that Justice O'Connor would treat it as inconsistent with the criteria she had advanced in case after case.

28. *Id.* at 24.
29. *Id.* at 31.

For their part, the Michigan lawyers were certain that
Bakke—never seriously challenged thanks to the White
House—would survive and with it, probably, their law
school admissions plan. They could certainly live with that,
indeed, they would be heroes of all academia. They could
also live with the loss of their two systems as long as *Bakke*
survived to provide a window for race-conscious admissions.
They might have added that in light of Texas, Florida, and
California, a loss would be more a blow to their pride than a
real setback for affirmative action.

It was clear from the day's argument that the early wisdom
favoring a reversal was probably wrong. Justice O'Connor at
least seemed disposed to embrace *Bakke*, or at least its essential permission of race-conscious admissions. Of course, we
could once again find that both the undergraduate and law
school programs had failed the *Bakke* test, but the intuition
of most observers went the other way. On the steps outside
following the argument, University President Mary Sue Coleman, who had succeeded Bollinger after he moved to Columbia, led supporters in a rousing rendition of "Hail to the
Victors." When she finished, Barbara Grutter peeled away
from Jennifer Gratz and Patrick Hammacher to respond to a
reporter asking how she felt. "I feel my life is hanging in the
balance waiting to hear if I will have equal justice under law,"
she replied.[30]

30. Liz Cobbs, *Powerful Hours Overtake Emotions at U.S. Supreme Court*,
ANN ARBOR NEWS, Apr. 2, 2003.

Chapter
Nine
Decision

Nothing better presaged the out-
come of the battle over Michigan's admission policies than
the quality of the legal pleadings placed before the Court. In
Grutter, the pivotal law school case, petitioner offered a competent, tightly bound statement of the law: *Bakke* is not bind-
ing because the critical section of Justice Powell's opinion
certifying diversity as a compelling need was disowned by
the four concurring justices who called it constitutional "at
least so long as the use of race to achieve an integrated student
body is necessitated by the lingering effects of past discrimination."[1] The law school admissions policies placed so
much emphasis on race that its "critical mass" formulation
was little more than a glorified quota. The state school had
failed to establish a compelling need for its race preference
policies because recent Court decisions had suggested that
the only compelling need it was prepared to recognize was
to provide redress for specific past discrimination. Moreover,

1. *Bakke*, 438 U.S. at 265, 326.

Michigan's approach was not narrowly tailored because it had failed to consider race-neutral alternatives to its policies.

Lacking in the petitions and briefs filed for *Grutter* was any overarching vision of where society was going and how the case at issue would impact on it. Lacking was any critique of the goal or educational value of engineered campus diversity, though fresh material was available in the form of an attitudinal survey taken by respected public opinion analysts Stanley Rothman, Seymour Martin Lipset, and Neil Nevitte[2] showing overwhelming campus opposition to race preferences among students, faculty, and administration, together with a correlation between the number of minorities on campus and sentiment among all three groups that race relations were poor. Two of Grutter's amici—the National Association of Scholars and the Center for Equal Opportunity—had effectively critiqued the Gurin Report purporting to show the "compelling need"[3] for campus diversity, but Grutter and her fellow victims needed their own theory of the case, and it was nowhere to be found. Not that their amici were wrong on the law or less than eloquent in their articulation of it. The Asian American Legal Foundation, for example, filed a moving brief recalling the historic discrimination to which Chinese Americans had been subjected and how many young Chinese students today are excluded from special elementary and secondary schools and programs because, as a group, they score so high on the entrance exams as to be judged insufficiently needy of the special resources offered by special schools. Now they find themselves rejected by elite universities in the name of diversity. "Social scientists may

2. Brief for the National Association of Scholars as Amicus Curiae Supporting Petitioner at 6, *Grutter v. Bollinger*, 123 S. Ct. 2325 (2003) (No. 02-241).
    3. *Id.*

debate how peoples' thoughts and behavior reflect their background, but the Constitution provides that the government may not allocate benefits or burdens among individuals based on the assumption that race or ethnicity determines how they act or think."[4] A nice statement of what the law should be, but without the compelling sense of social urgency the Michigan amici briefs would provide.

Also absent was a sense of unity between Petitioner and her most important amicus, the U.S. government. Grutter, by implication at least, was asking the Court to reverse the *Bakke* holding by declaring the nonvalidity of diversity as a compelling state interest. But the Bush administration was unwilling to go that far.

In his January 15, 2003, statement announcing the U.S. position in the case, the president ventured teasingly near a position denouncing race preferences: "At the law school, some minority students are admitted to meet percentage targets while other applicants with higher and better scores are passed over. This means that students are being selected or rejected based primarily on the color of their skin. The motivation for such an admissions policy may be very good, but its result is discrimination and that discrimination is wrong."[5] However, the administration's position before the Court was somewhat more circumspect. Its brief was more an advertisement for the percentage plans of Texas, California, and Florida than an exposition of the law as it was or ought to be. No argument at all was made for striking down diversity as a compelling need. Rather, the Court could do

4. Brief for the Asian American Legal Foundation et al., as Amicus Curiae Supporting Petitioner at 24, *Grutter v. Bollinger*, 123 S. Ct. 2325 (2003) (No. 02-241).

5. *Transcript of Bush's Remarks on Affirmative Action Policies*, NEW YORK TIMES, Jan. 16, 2003, at A26.

everything by doing virtually nothing: "In the end, this case requires this Court to break no new ground to conclude that respondents' race-based admissions policy is unconstitutional. This Court has long recognized that the Equal Protection Clause outlaws quotas under any circumstances and forbids the government from employing race-based policies when race-neutral alternatives are available. Those two cardinal principles of equal protection each suffice to invalidate respondents' race-based policy."[6]

If Ms. Grutter's case turned on the willingness of five justices to entertain the three percentage plans as a viable and constitutional alternative to the race-conscious policies of Michigan, it is small wonder that the Court would back the university.

Another example of the free-form nature of the *Grutter* amici briefs occurs in the brief filed by the Center for New Black Leadership, a conservative group long associated with the antipreference cause.[7] Throughout the litigation, the issue of black-white academic achievement gap—beginning before kindergarten, accelerating through years K–12, lingering through college and graduate school—was of central concern. The Center's brief cited many of the familiar statistics. For example, 63 percent of black and 56 percent of Hispanic fourth-graders "are below the most basic proficiency levels in reading." By age 17, the black is an average of four academic years behind whites in reading, 3.4 years in mathematics, 3.3 years in writing, four years in science. In 1995, the average white score on the SAT verbal exam was 448, compared to 356 for blacks; in quantitative reasoning it was

6. Brief for the United States at 10, *Grutter*.
7. Brief for the Center for New Black Leadership as Amici Supporting Petitioner, *Grutter v. Bollinger*, 123 S. Ct. 2325 (2003) (No. 02-241).

498 to 388. That same year among those scoring 700–800 in verbal ability, 8,978 were white, 1,476 were Asian Americans, and 184 were black. Among those scoring 750 or over in math, 9,519 were white, 3,827 were Asian Americans, and 107 were black. Among the 734 "superstar" students named by the College Board in 1995 as advanced placement scholars, 63.1 percent were white, 29.7 percent were Asian Americans, and only two individuals were black. Since the late 1980s, the gaps have been widening.[8] Despite their familiarity, the numbers continue to shock. But what is the root cause? And what is to be done? The Center asserted that the problem lies with K–12 education and "the concentration of economically disadvantaged black and Hispanic students in defective inner-city public schools."[9] And, of course, "Racial preferences do nothing to close that gap."[10] One might suggest that percentage plans, embraced in the Center brief, do nothing to close that gap either. Since the Court had no ability to address K–12 educational deficiencies and could deal only indirectly with percentage plans, there was no real response it could make to the terrible numbers problem.

It is instructive to compare how the respondents played the numbers game in their brief.

> In 1997 when petitioner applied, there were only 67 minority applicants, compared to 1,236 white and Asian American applicants, in the LSAT range (164+) from which over 90 percent of the admitted white students was drawn. Competition for these minority applicants is extremely fierce, and the Law School cannot hope to enroll more than a few of them. In 2000, there were only 26 African-American applicants *nationwide* with at least a 3.5 GPA and a 165 on

8. *Id.* at 6.
9. *Id.*
10. *Id.*

the LSAT compared to 3,173 whites and Asian Americans. Thus removing the race factor from admission consideration would have a devastating effect upon diversity at Michigan and other selective law schools. Unrebutted testimony at trial revealed that in one recent and typical year genuinely race-neutral admissions would have produced a class with 16 African Americans instead of the 58 who actually enrolled. Alternative systems such as a lottery for all those over some minimum LSAT score would effectively decapitate the class, removing most of the best students and—as more whites who do not now apply to the school learned about the softer standards and applied—the method would barely improve minority prospects from what they would be if an honest race-neutral system was applied.[11]

Nationwide, the effect would be identical to Michigan and disastrous for blacks. Citing a study published in a 1997 NYU *Law Review*, respondent argued that if the nation's law schools chose to maintain current academic standards but were barred from taking race into account in admissions, "the representation of African American students at the 89 most selective law schools would fall from approximately 7% now to less than 1%. Three-quarters of the African-American students who are currently admitted to accredited law schools would not be accepted *anywhere*, and 40% of those still admitted would be admitted only to schools with predominantly minority student populations."[12]

Clearly such an event would shake the landscape like a massive earthquake, confronting schools with the choice of compromising academic standards or losing nearly all their minority students. This was the best argument for declining to overrule *Bakke*, which has been the lighthouse on the

11. Respondent's Brief on the Merits, *Grutter v. Bollinger*, 123 S. Ct. 2325 (2003) (No. 02-241).

12. *Id.* at 37.

scene for the past twenty-five years, guiding universities through the rocky shoals of affirmative action law. Disturb it now, and imperil much in higher education that has been working well. This was a powerful argument requiring Justice O'Connor and the others to consider carefully the impact of their decision. The argument was coordinated masterfully with the interventions of amici from other sectors of society and the economy, each pleading the importance of diversity to its ability to perform its function in an evolving majority of minorities nation and the world beyond. We have already seen how the Green Brief weighed upon the justices during oral argument, as distinguished military veterans proclaimed the vital interest of their service in a diverse officer corps and the need for affirmative action in college ROTC and service academy admissions to ensure an adequate flow of such officers through the pipeline. This latest argument was the rest of the payoff from Bollinger's big theme strategy as other representatives of the "Great American Establishment" weighed in.

General Motors, the first great corporation—388,000 employees globally and annual revenues exceeding $175 billion—to enter the case, told the court it required students from elite schools able to deal confidently across great cultural divides. "A ruling proscribing the consideration of race and ethnicity in admissions decisions likely would dramatically reduce the diversity at our Nation's top institutions and thereby deprive students who will become the corps of our Nation's business elite of the interracial and multicultural interactions in an academic setting that are so integral to their acquisition of cross-cultural skills."[13]

The American Council on Education (ACE), representing

13. Brief of General Motors Corporation as Amicus Curiae in Support of Respondents at 3, *Grutter v. Bollinger*, 123 S. Ct. 2325 (2003) (No. 02-241).

about 1,800 colleges and universities, noted the exalted status of American institutions of higher learning on the world stage and claimed that much of this was due to the tradition of independence from government interference, particularly in areas once cited by Justice Felix Frankfurter as the "'four essential freedoms' of a university—to determine for itself on academic grounds who may teach, what may be taught, how it shall be taught, and who may be admitted to study."[14] As to the subject at hand, "Particular deference is owed educators' judgment about education because such matters require evaluation of cumulative information for which those responsible for higher education are best qualified. [Citation omitted] How, for example, the mix of students affects learning involves considerations educators are best equipped to gage. Such judgments require knowledge of campus and classroom dynamics, cognitive processes, how to nurture students' capacity for moral reasoning, and other specialized knowledge in which educators are trained."[15]

The American Bar Association (ABA), representing 400,000 lawyers nationwide, noted that in 1998, African Americans and Hispanics together accounted for only 7 percent of the nation's lawyers. Only with respect to dentists (4.8 percent) and scientists (6.9 percent) was the representation sparser. A ruling against Michigan would further reduce these numbers with extremely deleterious effects. "First, diversity of the bar is essential to fulfilling the legal profession's paramount purpose of providing representation to all.

14. Brief of American Council on Education and 52 Other Higher Education Organizations as Amici Curiae in Support of Respondents at 7, *Grutter v. Bollinger*, 123 S. Ct. 2325 (2003) (No. 02-241).
15. *Id.* at 11.

Second, diversity is fundamental to fostering the public's perception that our legal system is fair, unbiased, and inclusive, thereby preserving and enhancing the public's trust and confidence in our system of government."[16]

Steelcase, Inc., the world's largest manufacturer of office furniture and equipment, joined with a group of giants—Dupont, Dow, Eli Lilly, Microsoft, Proctor and Gamble, to name a handful—urging affirmation of the Sixth Circuit decision.[17] The common theme was similar to that articulated by General Motors: Corporate America is committed to a management that reflects, values, and implements the kind of diversity that has become an integral part of the corporate culture. Future corporate leadership is recruited from highly selective schools, such as Michigan. Deprive African Americans and other minorities of the opportunity to attend elite schools, and you deprive them of the chance to fully participate in the economy of today and tomorrow, while also depriving business of the benefits of the participation of minorities in management.

The argument is porous in the extreme. First and foremost, given the fact that Michigan's fate hinged on the willingness of the Court to sustain Justice Powell's opinion in *Bakke*, in arguing the need to sustain or increase the number of minorities in elite schools and professions, the school and its amici were running into the teeth of an argument Powell had rejected, saying that an interest in "reducing the historic deficit of traditionally disfavored minorities in medical schools and in the medical profession" represented an

16. Brief of the American Bar Association as Amicus Curiae in Support of Respondents at 6, *Grutter v. Bollinger*, 123 S. Ct. 2325 (2003) (No. 02-241).

17. Brief of 65 Leading American Businesses as Amici Curiae in Support of Respondents, *Grutter v. Bollinger*, 123 S. Ct. 2325 (2003) (No. 02-241).

unlawful interest in racial balancing.[18] Even had the question
been an open one, the link between affirmative action and
black economic advancement is, as even adherents of affirmative action concede, more an article of faith than a product
of evidence. Further, apart from those minorities who need
no affirmative action to succeed, there are few examples of
blacks rising to the top of the corporate or professional world.
Nor did any of the amici make a case as to why blacks and
other favored minorities graduating from higher positions in
not quite so selective schools could not contribute the same
diversity of thought and experience as they could graduating
from the bottom percentiles of more elite universities. Even
at the great universities, one could readily defend the proposition that sixteen fully qualified blacks in a law school class
would do more to destroy stereotypes and erase prejudice
than would be the case by adding forty-two affirmative
action–admitted students, using their race as both a sword
and a shield against classmates who know they would not be
at Michigan had racial preferences not intervened in the
admissions process. Finally, one must question the justification for race preferences based on the globalization of the
economy. Clearly, it is advantageous to have people at corporate headquarters familiar with the customs and traditions
of overseas societies. But a look at the nation's major trading
partners shows China, Japan, Taiwan, as well as several other
Asian states, Canada, Mexico, Central and South America,
and Europe. Of citizens with ethnic ties to these places, affirmative action on university campuses discriminates *against*
all except Mexican Americans. Even island Puerto Ricans
fail to pass Michigan's ethnic preference litmus test, though
it's hard to say why their contribution to diversity would be

18. *Bakke*, 438 U.S. at 306.

less than a former resident of San Juan now living in New York, Chicago, or Grand Rapids. Still, there was no doubt that Bollinger's strategic decision to sell *Bakke* as a doctrine long and fully internalized by progressive society proved a stroke of genius. With the Center for Individual Rights and its team narrowly focused on legal principles, which, however sound, had never been unconditionally embraced by the Court, Michigan's ability to preempt the sociological case would prove decisive.

Waiting for the Court

The author visited the Ann Arbor campus as the Supreme Court term was nearing its end with a decision expected any day. Several interviews had been suggested by the public affairs department, others came about through the author's own contacts.

In early summer, the law school was holding classes, and the campus churned with more student life than would be true at most universities. Law professors involved in the litigation were confident but not smug. They felt the school's admissions practice was close enough to the Harvard Plan endorsed by Justice Powell in *Bakke* to win sanction unless the Court chose to reverse *Bakke*, something not even the solicitor general had urged. Moreover, their sociological evidence had been effectively unrebutted, with the exception of some amici attacks on the Gurin Report. No one said so in so many words, but there was the impression that the undergraduate admissions procedure, with its automatic twenty-point bonus, had become something of a sacrificial lamb. The lawyers could defend the practice because the volume of undergraduate decisions was so many times that of the law school that a shorthand system could be justified. But they could also see a "swing justice" finding one plan consistent with *Bakke* and the other, not—a result they could easily live with. Bringing a system into compliance with a judicially sanctioned procedure was not all that difficult. Adjusting to a decision banning race-conscious decisions except to remedy past discrimination would be a serious burden. They believed the university is a progressive institution in a progressive state. True, residential discrimination has a long history in the area. Racial antagonisms surfaced in the unionization period of the 1930s, in the Southern black migration to jobs on the assembly lines during and after World War II, and in the urban riots of the 1960s. There had been opposition to busing for purposes of school integration during the 1970s. However, the stratification of Michigan society was more industrial than racial, and there had never been a period of de jure segregation.

The center of campus, known as the Diag, is where many of the pro-affirmative action rallies were held since the lawsuits were filed in 1997. Often the organizers were the Coalition to Defend Affirmative Action by Any Means Necessary (BAMN)—the term "by any means necessary" borrowed from the call to action by Malcom X. A conservative graduate recalled that the speakers rarely addressed the benefits of diversity. Rather, race preferences were sold as a matter of justice to atone for centuries of injustice. He said his former journal, *The Review*, covered a number of such rallies. One, dated October 11–25, 2000, reported on a Diag rally where the speaker called CIR "wrong" and "racist" for leading the pack against race preferences. Another heralded the cause as "equality, and to restart the civil rights movement."[19] Before long, the same rally had moved to touch other high visibility

19. Ryan Painter, *Who Are the Real Racists?* 20 MICH. REV., Oct. 10, 2000.

issues—campus rape, sexual harassment, even advice for blacks on the curriculum. Choose only courses from the Comprehensive Studies Program, the speaker urged, recommending a basic curriculum long on social and political subjects. Engineering and other more technical areas were not recommended because "[a] minority cannot go to the others and do well." A single "student mother" also spoke at the rally. She said the CIR agenda includes preventing women "from suing rappers [sic] and defending sexual harassment." The conservative recommended that the author visit the student union "where the tables are self-segregated."[20] However, the summer crowd was too light to prove or disprove the self-segregation charge.

A black student, who had been recommended by the university administration as a smart and articulate young man, returned the author's message. A recent graduate, he was now returning to work on a masters degree in sociology. He was tackling a tough issue in his studies—the gap between blacks and whites in educational achievement. He said that his thesis will declare the problem to be "structural." The student expounded on his thesis:

> It is not due to any genetic disability of black people. Nor is the essential cause environmental—single parenthood, high crime areas, inadequate schools, and the like, though obviously any of these conditions can influence the performance of affected students. Instead the cause is white prejudice. It cuts across all income levels and school racial compositions. Teachers and school administrators are simply prejudiced against black students. They steer them into the least challenging academic programs. Once that sort of tracking occurs, the process is reinforcing. With white children racing ahead on academic tracks, the black kids are

20. *Id.*

left behind. The gap between them increases with the years. The prejudice goes even further. A white student who misbehaves is assumed to have a treatable problem. A black student who misbehaves is thought to be incorrigible. They give up on him. The school—if he is allowed to remain in it—becomes for him nothing more than a custodial institution.

Why don't more black parents insist their sons and daughters be placed on the faster track, complete with AP courses?

Because they are too respectful of authority. Studies show black parents have far more respect for educators than white parents do. When they are told something about their children, they believe it. It's true no matter what the school. I went to a prestigious New England prep school. My parents are middle class. And do you know, all my teachers thought I was there to play football. They couldn't imagine me being serious about books. In fact, I felt so beaten down, my studies suffered. They thought I had a learning disability. My parents nearly pulled me out of school before I told them I could do the work. Then when I told my advisor I wanted to apply to Michigan, they said, "No, don't do it. You may get in, but you'll never be able to keep up with the work there."

Did you find the same attitude when you arrived?

Yes, it's systemic.

Does it have anything to do with affirmative action?

Maybe, but it begins at birth and ends at death. Affirmative action doesn't cause the attitudes that start before school and accompany you through college. In fact, affirmative action is the first chance you have to be treated as an equal after experiencing the downside of being black all your life. It is not a gift bestowed on us by white people. It is a small down payment on justice. We should take advantage of it without apology.

Are you glad you came to Michigan?

> It was the best decision of my life. It put the resources of a great university at my disposal. I can look at all the people who doubted I could do it and show them that I know that they know why they doubted me.

The black law student, whose friend, a white professor, acquainted the author with a letter from the student discussing his situation, was two-thirds through his first year of law school when a colleague urged him to apply for the *Law Review*, the prestigious journal of legal analysis that is considered a ticket to jobs clerking for important judges or working for the best and the brightest law firms. In most cases, only those at the upper reaches of each class are invited to compete, and only those whose ability to research and write in the scholarly but fluent manner of legal scholarship make the final cut. However, the student soon discovered that under the *Law Review's* affirmative action program, black competitors did not have to come from the upper reaches of the class as long as their grades were not "below a threshold to be determined by the Editor-in-Chief and the Managing Editor." Nor did their legal writing have to be distinguished, merely above "a zero on the Writing Competition." Affronted by the potential stigma of being judged an affirmative action *Law Review* member, the student declined to check the "Black" box on his application. On the basis of merit, he was invited to compete and awarded a place on the review. Still he was not mollified. For all the benefits of giving minorities a chance, increasing the number of black voices in legal literature, and providing an opportunity for those whose real abilities were repressed by prior discrimination, he urged that the policy should be changed. Minorities who were given their places through affirmative action "have a dubious credential in the struggle for competitive employment." Minority *Law Review* students also "face subtle and explicit doubt in the eyes of non-Review students" and hostility from those white students who applied but were not accepted. Those minorities who declined to enter through affirmative action channels face a particular irony in that "we are as qualified as white members but nobody knows it." The student added: "Personally, I am tired of having my achievements doubted." When he gained acceptance to the UM Law School, many thought he owed his acceptance to being black. "Finally, with the *Law Review*, I thought I could attain recognition for my merit rather than my color. Unfortunately, my membership is tainted." The letter to his professor friend was written in 1992. More than a decade later, the *Law Review* affirmative action policy persists.

Justice O'Connor's Day

On June 23, 2003, Justice O'Connor delivered the opinion of the Court in *Grutter v. Bollinger*, the law school case. After a summary of the facts, Justice O'Connor reviewed, at some length, Justice Powell's *Bakke* opinion, particularly his holding that race can be "a single though important element" in the consideration of the contribution an applicant might make to the university community. While declining to apply the *Marks v. United States* precedent, which would have bound the court to the Powell opinion on the theory that it was the narrowest, she nonetheless effusively endorsed the substance of Powell's views, including his central holding "that student body diversity is a compelling state interest that can justify the use of race in university admissions."[21] Given

21. *Grutter v. Bollinger*, 123 S. Ct. 2325, at 2337 (2003).

the equivocal nature of the Bush administration's intervention and its contagious influence upon the presentation of
Grutter's argument, it is hard to see how a majority could
have wound up anywhere else on that question.

What about earlier O'Connor pronouncements in *Metro
Broadcasting*, *Croson*, and *Adarand* suggesting, as directly
as the English language can, that only prior discrimination
and not diversity can provide a compelling interest sufficient
to constitute a compelling need? Cutely, Justice O'Connor
conceded that her own prior words might create that impression, "[b]ut we have never held that the only governmental
use of race that can survive strict scrutiny is remedying past
discrimination."[22] In other words, We said it, but we didn't
mean it. Or at least, we didn't hold it, and we are thus not
bound by it.

The next chunk of the decision serves as a monument to
the success of Bollinger's strategy of mobilizing the educational, business, legal, even military establishments behind
affirmative action. Paying little heed to her own past reasoning, O'Connor always found her way back to the position of
society's elites. Indifferent as she had been during her years
on the Court to the prerogatives of lower courts and other
branches of government, in *Grutter*, she displayed unusual
obedience to the whims of Big Education and its myriad
allies.

"The Law School's educational judgment that such diversity is essential to its educational mission is one to which we
defer," she wrote. "The Law School's assessment that diversity will, in fact, yield educational benefits is substantiated
by respondents and their *amici*. Our scrutiny of the interest
asserted by the Law School is no less strict for taking into

22. *Id.* at 2339.

account complex educational judgments in an area that lies primarily within the expertise of the university."[23] Also within the school's prerogative was the size of the minority force needed to achieve the intended benefits. If the school defined that size as a "critical mass," so be it. Both Michigan's own studies and the briefs of the amici show that in terms of students, substantial diversity "promotes learning outcomes and 'better prepares students for an increasingly diverse workforce and society and better prepares them as professionals' (citation omitted)."[24]

O'Connor continued: "These benefits are not theoretical but real, as major American businesses have made clear that the skills needed in today's increasingly global marketplace can only be developed through exposure to widely diverse people, cultures, ideas and viewpoints."[25] The identical perspective was offered by former senior members of the uniformed and civilian defense establishment who offered that a racially diverse officer corps "is essential to the military's ability to fulfill its mission to provide national security."[26] For all these reasons, O'Connor reasoned, "Effective participation by members of all racial and ethnic groups is essential if the dream of one Nation, indivisible is to be realized."[27]

Next, Justice O'Connor turned to the special role that universities in general and law schools in particular play as a training ground for the nation's political leadership. More than half the country's governors, half its senators, and a third of its House of Representatives come from the legal profession. "A handful of these schools account for 25 of the 100

23. *Id.*
24. *Id.* at 2340.
25. *Id.*
26. *Id.*
27. *Id.* at 2341.

United States Senators, 74 United States Court of Appeals judges, and nearly 200 of the more than 600 United States District Court judges."[28] To support the proposition that the "right" law schools make all the difference, Justice O'Connor cited the 1950 case of *Sweatt v. Painter*,[29] involving a black man excluded from the University of Texas Law School—the only public law school in the state—solely on the basis of race. When the Court ruled that Sweatt could not be denied an education by the state, Texas opened a second, and second-rate, law school exclusively for blacks with neither a library nor its own faculty. This action was overturned when the Court, which compared the status, resources, faculty, and alumni network of the two schools, concluded that separate but equal was in this case not equal at all. The *Sweatt* case is a far cry from *Grutter v. Bollinger*, where whites were excluded to make room for less-qualified blacks; where plaintiff was asking, as had Mr. Sweatt, that race be excluded as a factor in admission; and where a "second-tier" law school, such as Detroit's Wayne State, may have a much more aggressive network inside Michigan than the University of Michigan, which sends three-quarters of its graduating class to practice in other states.

It is also not at all clear that the same advantages that accrue to graduates of elite universities would be present if the superstructure of merit supporting each edifice were to be structurally compromised, particularly as regards the beneficiaries of that compromise. Institutional decisions, especially with respect to state universities, enjoy a presumption of fairness, which may be critical to their continued generous public backing.

28. *Id.*
29. *Sweatt v. Painter*, 339 U.S. 629 (1950).

On the issue of narrow tailoring, Powell's guidance was tricky and obtuse—the sort of judicial circumlocution that might have been the stuff of comedy had anyone understood it well enough to laugh. To pass constitutional scrutiny, Powell wrote, and O'Connor recalled, a system "cannot insulate each category of applicants with certain desired qualifications from competition with all other applicants."[30] Race can be a "plus" in a particular applicant's file, but not so as to "insulate the individual from comparison with all other candidates for the available seats."[31] The program, therefore, must be "flexible enough to consider all pertinent elements of diversity in light of the particular qualifications of each applicant, and to place them on the same footing for consideration, although not necessarily according them the same weight."[32]

If Powell's artful construction means anything, it means that individuals may have their race or ethnicity considered, sometimes heavily so, in terms of their ability to contribute to the diversity of campus viewpoint and experience. For this to evolve into a scheme to accumulate a "critical mass" of a handful of favored minorities—most of them individuals from comfortable backgrounds and with academic credentials a standard deviation or more below the mean of admitted whites and Asians—is to ridicule the principle of stare decisis while purporting to endorse it. But this is just what Justice O'Connor did, with the benediction, "We find that the Law School's admissions program bears the hallmarks of a narrowly tailored plan."[33] According to O'Connor, the program

30. *Bakke*, 438 U.S. at 316.
31. *Id.* at 317.
32. *Id.*
33. *Grutter*, 123 S. Ct. at 2342.

appears to be "flexible enough to ensure that each applicant is evaluated as an individual and not in a way that makes an applicant's race or ethnicity the defining feature of his or her application."[34]

Justice O'Connor was more convincing in rejecting the suggestion that Michigan's plan must fail because the Law School failed to seriously consider race-neutral alternatives. "We disagree," she wrote. "Narrow tailoring does not require exhaustion of every conceivable race-neutral alternative. Nor does it require a university to choose between maintaining a reputation for excellence or fulfilling a commitment to provide educational opportunities to members of all racial groups."[35] The Bush administration brief was not persuasive in demanding consideration of the percentage plans of Texas, Florida, and California. According to O'Connor, "The United States does not, however, explain how such plans could work for graduate and professional schools. Moreover, even assuming such plans are race-neutral, they may preclude the university from conducting the individualized assessments necessary to assemble a student body that is not just racially diverse, but diverse along all the qualities valued by the university."[36] Here the Court was only half right. Percentage plans only work, if at all, for undergraduate admissions, and, unless seriously doctored, they can result in a far less academically qualified class. On the other hand, the Court was hardly in a position to fret about the lack of real diversity epitomized by percentage plans given the artificial diversity in Michigan's admission schemes.

Justice O'Connor was clearly bothered by the timeless

34. *Id.* at 2343.
35. *Id.* at 2344.
36. *Id.* at 2345.

quality of the plan that she had approved. Indeed, far more than remedies for past discrimination, the pursuit of diversity is, by definition, a perpetual interest that must be satisfied by race preferences in admissions until such time as the gap in academic credentials narrows substantially. Limiting the remedy to a period of years would thus have been self-defeating. Therefore, Justice O'Connor, noting that twenty-five years had passed since the *Bakke* ruling, chose to close the body of her opinion with a more ambiguous declaration: "We expect that 25 years from now, the use of racial preferences will no longer be necessary to further the interest approved today."[37]

"Critical Mass"

Neither in brief nor in argument had the law school explained why the "critical mass" of African Americans was so much higher than that of Hispanics and so vastly much higher than Native Americans. This disparity was an important point. After all, if the purpose of achieving that critical mass was to avoid feelings of isolation among minorities, or to avoid making them feel as though they have to be spokespersons for their race, or to achieve the positive benefits of student interaction, it stands to reason that the numbers of admitted blacks, Hispanics, and Native Americans ought to be pretty much alike.

Chief Justice Rehnquist, writing for the four dissenting justices, charged that the majority's failure to explore the disparity between word and deed was inexcusable: "Although the Court recites the language of our strict scrutiny analysis, its application of that review is unprecedented in

37. *Id.* at 2347.

its deference."[38] Reviewing application and admissions figures for 1995 through 2000, Justice Rehnquist produced
charts showing that the percentage of blacks in the applicant
pool, which ran from 7.1 percent to 9.4 percent, was substantially mirrored by the percentage of blacks among those
admitted (7.3 percent to 9.7 percent). For Hispanics and
Native Americans, the trends were virtually identical. Hispanics ranged from 3.8 to 5.0 percent of the applicant pool
and 4.2 to 5.1 percent of those admitted; Native Americans,
from 0.7 to 1.1 percent of the pool, and 1.0 to 1.6 percent of
those admitted.[39] The law school's disparate treatment of
these minority group applicants "demonstrate[s] that its
alleged goal of 'critical mass' is simply a sham," wrote Rehnquist. "The Law School has managed its admissions program,
not to achieve a 'critical mass,' but to extend offers of admission to members of selected minority groups in proportion to
their statistical representation in the applicant pool. But this
is precisely the type of racial balancing that the Court itself
calls 'patently unconstitutional.'"[40]

It is noteworthy that Rehnquist based his dissent not on
the obsolescence of the *Bakke* standards but on their violation. Justice Kennedy, whose lonely dissenting opinion was
nonetheless important because he is closer to the center of
the Court on affirmative action issues than anyone save
Justice O'Connor, was even more emphatic in endorsing the
continuing viability of *Bakke*. "The opinion by Justice Powell, in my view, states the correct rule for resolving this case.
The Court, however, does not apply strict scrutiny. By trying
to say otherwise, it undermines both the test and its own

38. *Id.* at 2366.
39. *Id.* at 2368.
40. *Id.* at 2369.

controlling precedents."[41] The majority confused deference to a university's empirically supported judgment that racial and ethnic diversity contributes to the educational environment with deference to the means the university used to achieve that goal. The search for a so-called critical mass "is a delusion used by the Law School to mask its attempt to make race an automatic factor in most instances and to achieve numerical goals indistinguishable from quotas."[42] Deferring to such practices, stated Kennedy, carries grave dangers: "Preferment by race, when resorted to by the State, can be the most divisive of all policies, containing within it the potential to destroy confidence in the Constitution and the idea of equality."[43]

Finally, Justice Kennedy had the temerity to expose the dirty little secret of campus diversity: In the words of Yale Law School professor Peter Schuck, many professors who are "affirmative action's more forthright defenders readily concede that diversity is merely the current rationale of convenience for a policy that they prefer to justify on other grounds."[44] More will be said on this subject in the final chapter. Suffice it to say that the typical affirmative action advocate favors the policy as a means of redressing nearly four centuries of indignity heaped upon black men and women. However, because the Supreme Court has foreclosed that route to remedial action, pro-affirmative action advocates have reached for diversity as a substitute. "This is not to suggest the faculties at Michigan and other law schools do not pursue aspirations they consider laudable and consistent

41. *Id.* at 2370.
42. *Id.* at 2371.
43. *Id.*
44. *Id.* at 2372.

with our constitutional traditions," Justice Kennedy wrote. "It is but further evidence of the necessity for scrutiny that is real, not feigned, where the corrosive category of race is a factor in decision making."[45]

The dissent of Justice Thomas, joined by Justice Scalia, has won praise even from his ideological critics, and deservedly so. In terms of intellectual passion, legal weight, and precision of argument, it stands alone among the day's opinions. In an age less burdened by political correctness and conformity, Thomas might well be recognized as a great black intellectual. Today, the voices of victimization, the excuse-mongers, the seekers of special treatment have read this fiercely independent thinker not only out of the debate, but also out of the race.

Thomas began by citing Frederick Douglass's injunction that what the Negro needs "is not benevolence, not pity, not sympathy, but simply *justice*."[46] He then took dead aim at Michigan's elitist admissions policy, which necessitated special treatment for the preferred minorities selected for their contribution to the classroom "aesthetic," even though "[r]acial discrimination is not a permissible solution to the self-inflicted wounds of this elitist admissions policy."[47] Thomas then forcefully presented the case that Michigan had no compelling interest in maintaining any public law school, let alone an elite one. Several states—Alaska, Delaware, Massachusetts, New Hampshire, and Rhode Island—maintain no accredited public law schools at all. In fact, only California, Texas, and Virginia maintain elite law schools on a par with Michigan. Further, although the University of Michigan grad-

45. *Id.*
46. *Id.* at 2350.
47. *Id.*

uates about 30 percent of the in-state law school graduates each year, only 6 percent of the state bar-takers are Michigan alumni. This is because only about 27 percent of each year's class is from the state and only 16 percent of the law school's graduates stay in Michigan to practice.[48] This is a powerful set of numbers, and it makes it hard to imagine any compelling interest on the part of Michigan in supplying Chicago, New York, and Los Angeles with lawyers. Moreover, the law school's claim of its need to discriminate is entitled to no judicial weight under strict scrutiny standards. Indeed, the entire First Amendment rationale for admissions discrimination, defined first in *Bakke* and applauded by Justice O'Connor, is misplaced because no case relied on as precedent by the Court allowed the assertion of one constitutional right to trample another.

Thomas chose to accept O'Connor's twenty-five-year projection as a hard deadline for phasing out racial preferences, but his notions of justice were not soothed. "For the immediate future, however, the majority has placed its *imprimatur* on a practice that can only weaken the principle of equality embodied in the Declaration of Independence and the Equal Protection Clause. . . . It has been nearly 140 years since Frederick Douglass asked the intellectual ancestors of the Law School to 'do nothing with us!' and the Nation adopted the Fourteenth Amendment. Now we must wait another 25 years to see this principle of equality vindicated."[49]

In his short dissent, Justice Scalia, joined by Justice Thomas, was characteristically sarcastic. The decision, he warned, would prove contagious. Private employers could now be praised, rather than criticized, "if they also 'teach'

48. *Id.* at 2354.
49. *Id.* at 2350.

good citizenship to their adult employees through a patriotic, all-American system of racial discrimination in hiring."[50] He predicted new lawsuits would erupt over particulars of the decision, parenthetically adding, "Tempting targets, one would suppose, will be those universities that talk the talk of multiculturalism and racial diversity in the courts but walk the walk of tribalism and racial segregation on their campuses—through minority-only student organizations, separate minority housing opportunities, separate minority student centers, even separate minority-only graduation ceremonies."[51]

The *Gratz* decision, written by Chief Justice Rehnquist, struck down the undergraduate admissions practice of awarding 20 points out of the 100 needed to guarantee admission for membership in a preferred minority group.[52] The Court held that the rigid practice was not narrowly tailored under Justice Powell's *Bakke* standard, which purported to demand the individualized consideration of race, along with other factors, in seeking a diverse class. Of course, Powell had also appended the Harvard Plan to his opinion, which underlines the importance of having sufficient numbers of minorities on campus to become a factor in the institutionalization of diversity. Having voted against *Bakke* in 1978, the Chief Justice was now employing it as the standard against which race-conscious admissions procedures must be judged. In a case that began amid great hopes by conservatives to see *Bakke* overturned, only Justices Thomas and Scalia seemed prepared to go in that direction. Justice O'Connor joined the majority opinion and also wrote a sep-

50. *Id.* at 2349.
51. *Id.* at 2350.
52. *Gratz v. Bollinger*, 123 S. Ct. 2411 (2003).

arate concurring opinion that was something of a victory lap at the time. Noting that the University of Michigan remains free to modify its system, she declared the current system to be "a nonindividualized, mechanical one" and thus outside the bounds of *Bakke*.[53]

O'Connor's long judicial journey on affirmative action, through union contracts and compensatory hiring schemes, broadcast licensing and government contracting preferences, had brought her and the Court back very close to where things were when she first took her place on the bench. As University of Michigan officials gave gleeful media interviews on the steps outside, those who believed O'Connor had been leading the Court from the shadows of racial stereotyping to the sunlight of equal protection were bitterly disappointed.

53. *Id.* at 2433.

Chapter
Ten

After
Michigan

On August 23, 2003, the University of Michigan announced it had adopted a new process for undergraduate admissions to replace the one that had been disallowed by the Supreme Court in *Gratz v. Bollinger.* Henceforth, there would be no point system, no fixed advantage applicable to each and every member of a preferred minority. Instead race would be one of many factors considered in an admissions process that will be "flexible, holistic and individualized." The school hired more than a dozen new readers to review applications and make a recommendation regarding the disposition of each one. A professional admissions counselor would then conduct a "blind reading" of the application and make his or her own recommendation.[1] The complete file would then be sent to a senior level manager in the office of university admissions. If there were disagreement over the case, the file would go to an admissions review committee for further consideration. The task of

1. University of Michigan Undergraduate Admissions Application, Guidelines and Process 2003–2004 (Regents of the University of Michigan).

assessing each applicant in this holistic manner would be facilitated by new essay questions designed to give the applicant more of an opportunity to describe his or her own special traits and influences. "Race will," in the words of an accompanying handout, "be only one of many additional factors taken into consideration during the review process, as will socioeconomic factors, geography, and special or unique experiences, skills and talents."[2] Not until at least the fall of 2004 will observers be able to begin to assess whether the new procedures provide a different outcome from that experienced under the outlawed system, namely the acceptance of every minority applicant minimally qualified to pursue the school's academic program. "I believe the new system will allow us to continue enrolling a student body that is both academically excellent and diverse in many ways," said Mary Sue Coleman, Bollinger's successor as university president.[3]

Striking by its absence from the new policy was any reference to the "critical mass" standard approved by the Court in *Grutter*, the companion law school case. This may be because the school has finally absorbed *Bakke*'s essential lesson: The more vague the standard, the less likely a successful legal challenge. It may also be that the school wants to avoid what may be called "the guffaw factor," a claim so transparently calculated to comply with the letter rather than the spirit of the law that it provokes laughter in any knowledgeable audience. The reason adapting the standard approved for the law school to the university as a whole might inspire such mirth would be its underlying assumption that the number of minorities needed to overcome stereotypes

2. *Id.*
3. *Id.*

and otherwise share perceptions with classmates based on experiences unique to a race or ethnic group varies in direct proportion to the size of the class. Sixty-eight blacks in a class of 500 means 680 to a class of 5,000—a number that even newly deferential Justice O'Connor might have a hard time swallowing. Even more troublesome would be the effort to apply the critical mass shibboleth to the entire range of academic disciplines. As critics have noted, ten African American students might well enliven a law school class dealing with constitutional law, civil rights litigation, or even trial practice. Transferring this concept to mechanical engineering, business accounting, or German 101, however, is a stretch.

Michigan was not the only school reevaluating its admissions procedures. The Supreme Court decisions affected every public college and university in the country and, via the Civil Rights Act of 1964, every private school receiving federal aid. A study published in 2001 by the Center for Equal Opportunity, using data provided by forty-seven public colleges and universities, concluded that race preferences were far more widely practiced and larger than had previously been appreciated, particularly at the most selective of the schools reviewed. The combined verbal-math white-black SAT difference was, for example, 180 points at the Naval Academy, 210 points at William and Mary, 230 points at the University of Michigan, and 330 points at UC-Berkeley.[4] By summer's end, these and other schools had been huddling with each other and with representatives of the Council on Higher Education to bring their programs into line with the *Bakke-Bollinger* standards. Under a program designed with little heed to *Bakke*, which refers to race as a potential tie-

---

4. Lerner & Nagai, *A Critique of the Expert Report of Patricia Gurin.*

breaker between two candidates of relatively equal credentials, not as a ladder for a barely qualified student to reach
the window of opportunity, those kinds of spreads might be
difficult to sell. Thus, even though the Court had upheld the
Michigan Law School operation, schools that had in place
systems similar to those struck down by the circuit courts in
Texas and Georgia could not look forward to vindication by
the Supreme Court.

In a sense, the most laudable opinions in the two cases
were Justice Thomas's dissent in *Grutter* and Justice Ruth
Bader Ginsburg's dissent in *Gratz*. Justice Thomas saw diversity as an illegitimate justification for riding roughshod over
the equal protection clause. Justice Ginsburg rejected the
claim of a majority of her colleagues that the discrimination
of inclusion and that of exclusion must be weighed on the
same scale. Racism still exists in the country, she maintained.
The deprivations born of slavery and segregation continue to
haunt our nation. "[T]o say that two centuries of struggle for
the most basic of civil rights have been mostly about freedom
from racial categorization rather than freedom from racial
oppression is to trivialize the lives and deaths of those who
have suffered under racism. To pretend . . . that the issue
presented in *Bakke* [citation omitted] was the same as the
issue in *Brown v. Board of Education* [citation omitted] is to
pretend that history never happened and that the present
doesn't exist."[5] Moreover, she said, the drive within the academic community to reach out to minorities is so pervasive
that attempts to limit or channel it will only bring about a
situation where "institutions of higher education may resort
to camouflage. For example, schools may encourage applicants to write of their cultural traditions in the essays they

5. *Gratz*, 123 S. Ct. at 2444 (2003).

submit, or to indicate whether English is their second language. Seeking to improve their chances for admission, applicants may highlight the minority group associations to which they belong, or the Hispanic surnames of their mothers or grandparents. In turn, teachers' recommendations may emphasize who a student is as much as what he or she has accomplished."[6] Justice Ginsburg was not manufacturing her examples from thin air. As she noted, in suggesting "race-neutral" alternatives to race preferences, the brief of the United States suggested schools could consider "a history of overcoming disadvantage," "reputation and location of high school," and "individual outlook as reflected by essays."[7] Justice Ginsburg warned, "If honesty is the best policy, surely Michigan's accurately described, fully disclosed College affirmative action program is preferable to achieving similar numbers through winks, nods, and disguises."[8]

Many scholars—even some firm supporters of affirmative action—have been highly skeptical of the emergence of diversity as its principal vehicle in academia. For example, Dean Anthony T. Kronman of the University of Florida said of diversity, "It is striking that a word which a generation ago carried no particular moral weight and had, at most, a modestly benign connotation, should in this generation have become the most fiercely contested word in American higher education."[9] Indeed, the NAACP, which during the 1950s and 1960s urged a policy of color-blindness, opposed early efforts at preferential hiring as "a crevasse which has no bot-

6. *Id.* at 2446.
7. *Id.*
8. *Id.*
9. Anthony T. Kronman, *Is Diversity a Value in American Higher Education?* 52 FLA L REV 861 (2000).

tom."[10] Peter Schuck of Yale Law School recites only the obvious when he noted, "[M]any of affirmative action's more forthright defenders readily concede that diversity is merely the current rationale of convenience for a policy that they prefer to justify on other grounds."[11]

Professor Samuel Issacharoff of Columbia, who spent eight years defending the University of Texas affirmative action program in the *Hopwood* case, sees diversity as a poor rationale for minority preferences. He wrote: "I have now spent the majority of my professional life in the academy and I have seen the concept of diversity enshrined at the highest levels of the academic pantheon. But in the endless discussions of diversity, I have never heard the term seriously engaged on behalf of a Republican, a fundamentalist Christian, or a Muslim."[12] If diversity is the goal, then limiting it to blacks, Mexican Americans, or Puerto Ricans—as long as they don't dwell on the island itself—is a farce, the only purpose of which is to avoid judicial rejection.

Diversity, of course, became the rationale of choice for colleges because, after the Supreme Court in *Wygant* ruled out societal discrimination as a justification for race preferences, the colleges were left with either the diversity claim from *Bakke* or trying to convince federal judges that the preferences were remedies for their own past discrimination. For thirty years running, any discrimination the schools practiced was on behalf of minorities rather than against them, so it was really a choice between the fabricated diversity ration-

10. Deborah C. Malamud, *Race, Culture, and the Law: Values, Symbols, and Facts in the Affirmative Action Debate*, 95 MICH. L. REV. 1668, 1674 (1997).

11. PETER H. SCHUCK, DIVERSITY IN AMERICA: KEEPING GOVERNMENT AT A SAFE DISTANCE 160 (2003).

12. Samuel Issacharoff, *Law and Misdirection in the Debate Over Affirmative Action*, 11 U. CHI LEGAL F 18 (2002).

ale and nothing. In grasping at the only straw available, the academic community appropriated a policy unconstrained by time, with beneficiaries, such as Hispanics, who had no reasonable claim to compensatory relief; with no demonstrated record of accomplishing anything positive; and with a history of mischief in its impact on academic processes.

Issacharoff made several telling points regarding diversity in academia. Academic officials are granted an unparalleled license to determine how much diversity is necessary, when clearly "[e]ach additional black enrollee brings diminishing marginal returns in terms of racial diversity."[13] After the school has a minimum number of blacks on campus, which is worth more in terms of diversity—the next black, or "the first Alaskan resident, or Christian fundamentalist, or Vietnamese immigrant, or former soap opera star, etc."?[14]

Choosing students for reasons of diversity degrades rather than serves the fundamental values of academia. Derek Bok, co-author of *The Shape of the River*, the prodiversity academic manifesto, had an entirely different perspective with respect to faculty appointments when he was president of Harvard. He wrote: "If selection committees decide to pass over the ablest candidates in order to appoint a minority scholar, they can scarcely be said to be furthering the primary educational aims of the institution. On the contrary, they will generally be acting with a clear probability of diminishing the quality of teaching and research."[15]

Many academicians also take exception to the confusion between racial or ethnic diversity and viewpoint diversity.

---

13. *Id.* at 25.
14. *Id.*
15. DEREK BOK, BEYOND THE IVORY TOWER: SOCIAL RESPONSIBILITIES OF THE MODERN UNIVERSITY 111 (1982).

To begin with, in the vast majority of classes—biology, civil procedure, differential calculus, for example—race and ethnicity are simply irrelevant. But what of other courses, such as constitutional law or civil rights? Writing in the Michigan *Law Review*, Terrance Sandalow recounted, "My own experience and that of colleagues with whom I have discussed the question, experience that concededly is limited to the classroom setting, is that racial diversity is not responsible for generating ideas unfamiliar to some members of the class. Students do, of course, quite frequently express and develop ideas that others in the class have not previously encountered, but even though the subjects I teach deal extensively with racial issues, I cannot recall an instance in which, for example, ideas were expressed by a black student that have not also been expressed by a white student."[16]

Sandalow is also among a growing number of academicians who make the case that affirmative action has been a substantial contributor to the process of grade inflation, which has increasingly undercut the integrity of the college classroom. Why have the two been linked? According to Sandalow, "Liberal guilt is one reason. Another is the fear that a high failure rate would adversely affect an institution's competitive position in the intense competition to attract the most promising African-American students. But other more justifiable reasons have also played a role. Many faculty members believe that it would be ethically problematic to admit students who will do less well than their classmates, inviting them to invest a year or more of their lives and perhaps substantial sums, and then fail them out of school."[17]

16. Terrance Sandalow, *Minority Preferences Reconsidered*, 97 Mich. L. Rev. 1874, 1903 (1999).
    17. *Id.* at 167.

Even had studies conclusively proven the linkage between the increased presence of preferred minorities on campus and positive academic outcomes, the constitutional case for diversity would still have been weak. Issacharoff came at the issue from an unorthodox but effective angle. Suppose it were shown that students learned better in a homogeneous environment because it provided fewer distractions and was less emotionally taxing. "Would any serious constitutional scholar claim that such reasoning would justify the use of racial classifications to reinforce segregation?"[18]

These were powerful arguments to be made in the courts but were, in the main, neglected by both CIR and the Justice Department. CIR put most of its stock into the claim that diversity had not been declared a compelling interest by the Court and that, in any event, it could be achieved by means more narrowly tailored than the law school's "critical mass" approach. Justice hurt the case by lauding diversity and assuring the Court that diversity could be achieved by the political hocus-pocus of percentage plans. Both established credentials as backers of plans specifically calculated to achieve racial and ethnic diversity, so long as the plans themselves were "race neutral." Given the importance of the amici briefs and their own purported compelling need for diversity, it is not obvious why the basis on which the need was asserted wasn't itself subjected to more careful scrutiny. Yes, all know the demographics of the country are changing, and yes, all are aware of the increasingly global nature of U.S. economic interests. However, there is now a vast body of literature, accumulated over forty years, of corporate diversity. Summarizing much of this literature in 1998, Katherine Y. Wil-

18. Issacharoff, *Law and Misdirection*, at 28.

liams and Charles A. O'Reilly III offered the following: "Research has documented that categorizing people into groups, even on trivial criteria, can lead members to perceive out-group members as less trustworthy, honest, and cooperative. . . . This process results in increased stereotyping, polarization and anxiety. In heterogeneous groups, these effects have been shown to lead to decreased satisfaction with the group, increased turnover, lowered levels of cohesiveness, reduced within-group communication, decreased cooperation, and higher levels of conflict."[19] The authors also stated: "Large amounts of diversity in groups may offer little in the way of added value from unique information and make group cohesion and functioning difficult."[20]

Corporations may embrace diversity out of a sense of public duty. They may advertise their diversity in markets that care deeply about such things. They may satisfy costly government oversight by developing affirmative action or diversity plans. They may make it more costly for competitors to enter the field knowing they may have to match expensive plans already in place. However, the weight of the literature is such that an amici could more credibly have argued a compelling interest in homogeneity rather than diversity. (Again, no one is recommending a reversion to the days of racial and ethnic discrimination.) The paradox could have been used to unmask the key argument of the university, because no sane person would argue that the burdens of diversity justify a policy of old-fashioned segregationist selectivity.

19. Katherine Y. Williams & Charles A. O'Reilly, *Demography and Diversity in Organizations: A Review of 40 Years of Research,* 20 RESEARCH IN ORGANIZATIONAL BEHAVIOR, 77, 84 (1998).
    20. *Id.* at 90.

Black Academic Performance

The strongest case for upholding Michigan's two admissions procedures had nothing to do with the law and everything to do with inadequate academic performance by blacks in this country. By now, the statistics that once shocked have become familiar. Several of those statistics were integrated carefully into the respondents' Supreme Court brief. Others can be easily obtained. Presented as they were on behalf of Bollinger, they amount to little more than a plea for mercy because merit would cut with cruelty. Whites, for example, are fourteen times as likely as blacks to achieve the combined verbal-math score of 1300 widely regarded as a minimum for acceptance to the nation's highly selective colleges. The mean LSAT scores for Harvard and Yale students in 1995–96 was 170, a figure reached by only seventeen black students in the United States.[21] No one has as yet offered a convincing explanation for this sorry story. Income? The lowest income quartile of whites outscores the highest quartile of blacks. Unfair standardized tests? The tests overpredict the performance of blacks in college or law school. More whites take the preparatory exams? In 1996–97, 28 percent of black students took an LSAT preparation course; their median score was 141.58. However, only 31 percent of whites took a preparation course for the exam, and their median score was 152.11.[22] What about the bad schools, the inadequate K–12 schooling? Yes, many inner-city schools are bad, at least in terms of student performance and some—far fewer than

21. Respondent's Brief on the Merits at 6, *Grutter v. Bollinger* (No. 02-241), 123 S. Ct. 2325 (2003).

22. Jack Greenberg, *Affirmative Action in Higher Education: Confronting the Condition and Theory*, 43 B.C.L. REV. 521, 553 (2002).

appears generally appreciated—in terms of resources. What about the blacks who attend the best suburban, or even private schools? They do better, certainly better than the inner-city blacks, but consider the case of Shaker Heights, Ohio, an upper-middle-class suburb of Cleveland. The town organized during the 1960s to establish and maintain an integrated community with top schools and other public amenities. In many respects, the community has been a relative haven for citizens who believe that, in the future, blacks and whites must live as neighbors. Yet the single intractable problem has been and remains the huge gap between black and white students from the elementary school level all the way through high school. On proficiency test scores for the year 1995, white fourth-graders scored 98 percent in math, 99 percent in reading, 95 percent in writing, and 94 percent in science. For blacks, the scores were 73 percent, 90 percent, 74 percent, and 51 percent, respectively. Among white sixth-graders, the scores were 86 percent in math, 97 percent in reading, 93 percent in writing, and 79 percent in science. For blacks, scores were 28 percent, 70 percent, 67 percent, and 21 percent, respectively. White eighth-graders scored 92 percent in math, 100 percent in reading, 93 percent in writing, and 91 percent in science. The respective black scores were 37 percent, 83 percent, 77 percent, and 48 percent. For black students, the mean SAT scores in 1996 were 485 verbal and 471 math. For whites, those scores were 600 verbal and 598 math.[23]

Both black and white parents were concerned and invited the distinguished black sociologist John U. Ogbu for an extended visit to the city and its schools. Ogbu found the

---

23. JOHN U. OGBU, BLACK AMERICAN STUDENTS IN AN AFFLUENT SUBURB 36 (2003).

most profound problem to be what he called "academic dis-engagement" by black students and, to some extent, their families. Compared with whites, blacks cared less about school, sought easier courses, did less homework, studied fewer hours, and were content to do just well enough to graduate and go onto college. Parents too were less involved with educational issues affecting their children than were white parents. Some felt the teachers were racist, others experienced a sense of low expectations, and many believed that taking advanced placement and other challenging courses was "a white thing."[24]

Now consider a University of Michigan admissions officer. He may have a number of applicants, both black and white, from Shaker Heights. That officer knows there will be a sliver of highly qualified blacks at the top of the class, and he also knows that Shaker Heights is about as good as it gets for a suburban public school district. He knows too that if he applies honest race-neutral standards, some of the blacks he turns away will wind up at other selective colleges, and he may be asked to explain why he "lost" them. Others will go to less-selective schools where they have a lesser chance of matriculating after four or even six years and a much lesser chance of going to graduate school. He is aware of the history of slavery and segregation, the centuries of Jim Crow and job discrimination, the white race riots when blacks sought to rent homes so they could work in defense plants during World War II, and the black rioting that followed Martin Luther King's murder in 1968. He also knows that in the year 2000, blacks, with 12 percent of the population, made up 48.8 percent of those arrested for murder and nonnegligent manslaughter, 53.9 percent of those arrested for robbery, and

24. *Id.* at 116.

34 percent of those arrested for aggravated assault. That same year, blacks constituted 50 percent of the two million jailed offenders. Current projections have 28 percent of black males serving time in state or federal prison during their lifetimes, compared with 4.4 percent of white males.[25] Is this officer likely to turn down the application of the "average" Shaker Heights black applicant and others like him, or is he going to find in this young student the prospect of contributing meaningfully to campus diversity at the University of Michigan? If he rejects this student and others like him, will he fuel the sense of academic disengagement among black students in Shaker Heights? Or will they slowly come to the realization that hard work, and not racial entitlement, is the way to make progress in this society? Making such a decision is a weighty burden for any school official to bear.

Moving Ahead

Those who have resisted race preferences in higher education, as in all other walks of American life, now confront the question of where to go after Michigan. The extraordinary battle waged at the direction of the university's former president Lee Bollinger reversed the march of precedent that had been gaining momentum against preferences based on race and succeeded in gaining judicial sanction for a precedent constrained by neither time nor workable standard, save— for a while anyway—the university's own discretion. Bollinger succeeded by attracting the vote of Justice Sandra Day O'Connor, who had previously been leading the judicial march in the opposite direction.

---

25. Jack Greenberg, *Affirmative Action in Higher Education: Confronting the Condition and Theory*, 43 B.C.L. REV. 521, 556 (2002).

The first option is simply to keep fighting in the courts. Few of the selective colleges and universities practicing affirmative action have programs that perfectly reflect the guidance first offered by Justice Powell in the form of the Harvard Plan and later endorsed by Justice O'Connor. Perhaps with the right case, the Court could tighten its standards. Perhaps a case filed today would not reach the Court until personnel changes have occurred. Dogged organizations like the Center for Individual Rights and others are supposed to fight like pit bulls for the right cause, and equal protection of the law is surely a cause worth fighting for.

There are, however, serious obstacles to proceeding in this fashion. For one thing, at least six and perhaps seven justices—depending on where one places Chief Justice Rehnquist—embraced *Bakke* in one *Bollinger* case or the other. The Court will almost certainly allow the dust to settle before getting back into the arena. It is likely to be many years before certiorari is granted on another diversity case involving higher education. Also, opponents of race preferences are themselves divided over certain key issues, never a good omen in terms of launching a reenergized campaign. How important is diversity to a major university? Should a school like Michigan be forced to choose between diversity and the highest academic standards? Should states be in the business of seeking racial information in the first place? Such prominent opponents of race-conscious policies as Thomas Wood and Ward Connerly are at loggerheads over these issues. Why further stress an important alliance?

One must also be concerned about what would be won, even if a new round of lawsuits proved more successful than the last. Such a victory would undoubtedly be met—as were the "victories" in California, Texas, and Florida—by a proliferation of facially race-neutral measures designed to restore the status quo ante before a particular program was abbreviated by referendum, statute, or executive action. The percentage plans that took hold in California, Texas, and Florida are being judged mainly by their ability to restore the minority student presence to levels enjoyed before the intervening event, what Justice Ginsburg called affirmative action through "winks, nods, and disguises."[26] This, in and of itself, is not objectionable if the minority students coming back represent a quantum leap in academic credentials over those previously admitted through affirmative action. But this is not happening because of the paucity of exceptional black students in the pipeline. Of course, at their best, the percentage plans do not reach graduate schools, which have their own forms of subterfuge. Consider the machinations of UCLA in the wake of Prop. 209. First it sought to reacquire a pre-209 minority presence by stuffing its admissions material with a ton of socioeconomic data on the student—family income, parents' education, single mother, quality of the applicant's neighborhood. Next it borrowed from India—that bastion of racial harmony—a notion called the "creamy layer" principle, trying to identify members of "castes" able to rise to the top like cream in a container of milk. UCLA has also recruited law students willing to study critical race theory, a black intellectual discipline wedded to the notion that blacks will benefit more by using political clout to get their fair share of the pot rather than by relying on the rule of law. Meanwhile, the president of the University of California at Berkeley has proposed terminating reliance on SATs, and Mexican American and other Spanish-speaking students are

---

26. *Gratz*, 123 S. Ct. at 2431.

seeking to have their fluency in Spanish recognized on the companion SAT 2 test.[27]

This is the predictable response of colleges and universities, perhaps aided by sympathetic legislatures to adverse court decisions. Fighting these "race-neutral" alternatives to affirmative action in the courts would require the same commitment and at least as much time as it took to strike down the assortment of segregationist dodges during the 1950s and 1960s. First came the resourceful pupil assignment plans, then the repeal of mandatory schooling legislation, then the "freedom of choice" plans, then the closing down of entire school systems, and so on. After more than a decade of "desegregation" following *Brown v. Board*, fewer than 3 percent of the black children in the states of the old Confederacy were attending integrated schools. Those who today support race preferences are as committed to their way of thinking as were the segregationists of the mid-century South. They are just as durable, and, although we may disagree with their methods, their underlying cause is infinitely more just. It is, in short, a potential court battle that will never end, that will bitterly divide antipreference forces, and that will never produce final victory or defeat. For that reason, the battle is probably not worth fighting.

A second option involves trying to achieve by referendum what was lost in the courts. Michigan would be one juicy target for a 209-type referendum. Other states may follow. The idea's strength is that it plays into the strength of public opinion, which in every reliable survey has shown itself against special preferences based on race. It is also more expeditious than a lawsuit, which takes years to fight and may wind up with a denial of certiorari. The downsides are enor-

27. Greenberg, *Affirmative Action in Higher Education*, at 521, 552.

mous, however. Such referenda are bitterly divisive. Experience in both Washington State and California makes it clear that though majorities opposed to race preferences can be mobilized for a single vote on the issue, they quickly return to their normal diffuse voting patterns, while the "losers" keep a grudge against the party they hold responsible for their defeat. For that reason, the Republican "pros" hate these referenda battles. Governor Jeb Bush's One Florida executive edict had, as its principal and successful mission, the goal of getting Ward Connerly, and the proposed referendum in his briefcase, out of his state. The referenda, also, of course, have nothing to do with the elaborate percentage plans, which could be expected to appear in the wake of a referendum or other action abolishing racial preferences. Again, the objection to such plans is not that they restore the relative racial numbers but that they do so in disguise, and also, that the relative academic credentials gap between majority and minority students has barely budged. So, in the end, race preference foes would likely be back where they started, with a fair amount of political ill will generated by their efforts. Small wonder many conservative officeholders would rather swallow preferences—disguised or otherwise—than referenda designed to shut them down.

I propose, instead, letting affirmative action go forward with one significant change and several reforms designed to ensure both transparency and "truth in packaging." Either by executive order or, if necessary, legislation, my plan would:

1. Permit all colleges and universities subject to federal jurisdiction under the equal protection clause or the Civil Rights Act to accept and enroll any number of affirmative action students they wish.

2. Require all such institutions to file with the U.S. Secretary

of Education timely and accurate records of all such admissions.

3. Maintain on "defer consideration" or waiting lists a sufficient number of applicants from nonpreferred racial or ethnic categories (mainly whites and Asian Americans) so as to be able to match the number of affirmative action enrollees on a one-for-one basis. We may call this group the "Equal Protection" list.

4. Admit and enroll in each entering class the identical number of "Equal Protection" applicants consisting of races not eligible for affirmative action as there are affirmative action admissions.

As a rule of thumb, U.S. Department of Education officials can assume that any class in which the difference in SAT (or the ACT equivalent) between blacks and Hispanics on the one hand and whites and Asian Americans on the other is 75 points or more, or high school GPA differences are 0.3 points or more, is one in which race preferences have been practiced, and, thus, ameliorative steps would be required.

This proposal takes its inspiration from an earlier generation of affirmative action cases, which tended to pay close attention to the hardship worked on innocent victims of race preferences. Admittedly, the courts in the employment cases were more protective of whites whose tenure or seniority were threatened rather than with white job applicants, but since a certain asymmetry exists between the employment and education spheres, the focus on student admissions seems appropriate. Colleges and universities would have to expand their facilities to accommodate an indeterminate number of additional students, but the additional tuition generated could ease any administrative pain. Had this proposal been in effect during the past several years, the entire diversity charade could have been eliminated, colleges and universities could have devoted more of their time to educating their students and less to organizing their campuses along ethnic and racial lines. Also instead of battling their way to the Supreme Court and lamenting the opportunities denied, Barbara Grutter, Jennifer Gratz, and Patrick Hammacher would have been studying at the University of Michigan.

Index